POP ART

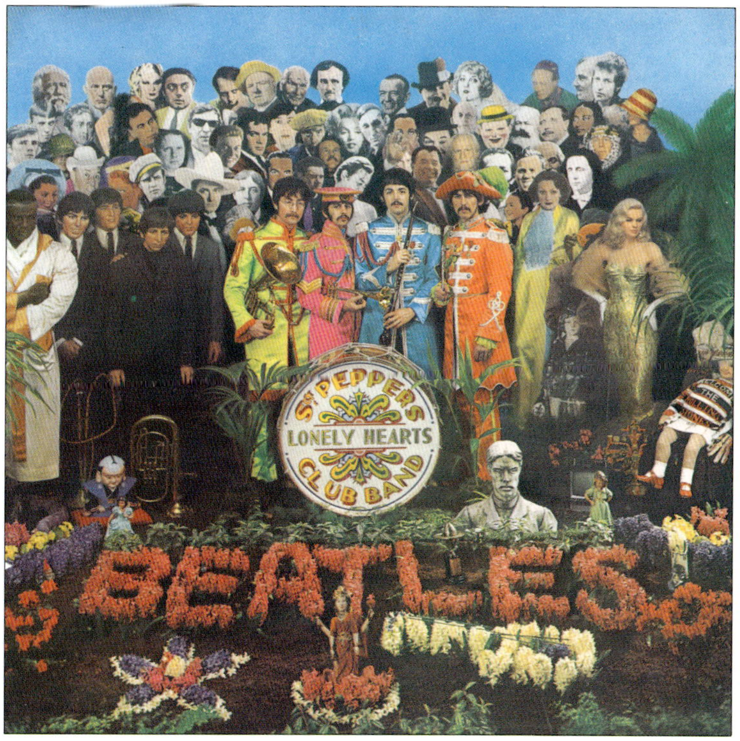

Peter Blake and Jann Haworth, Sgt Pepper Album Cover. © *Apple Corps Ltd, 1967*

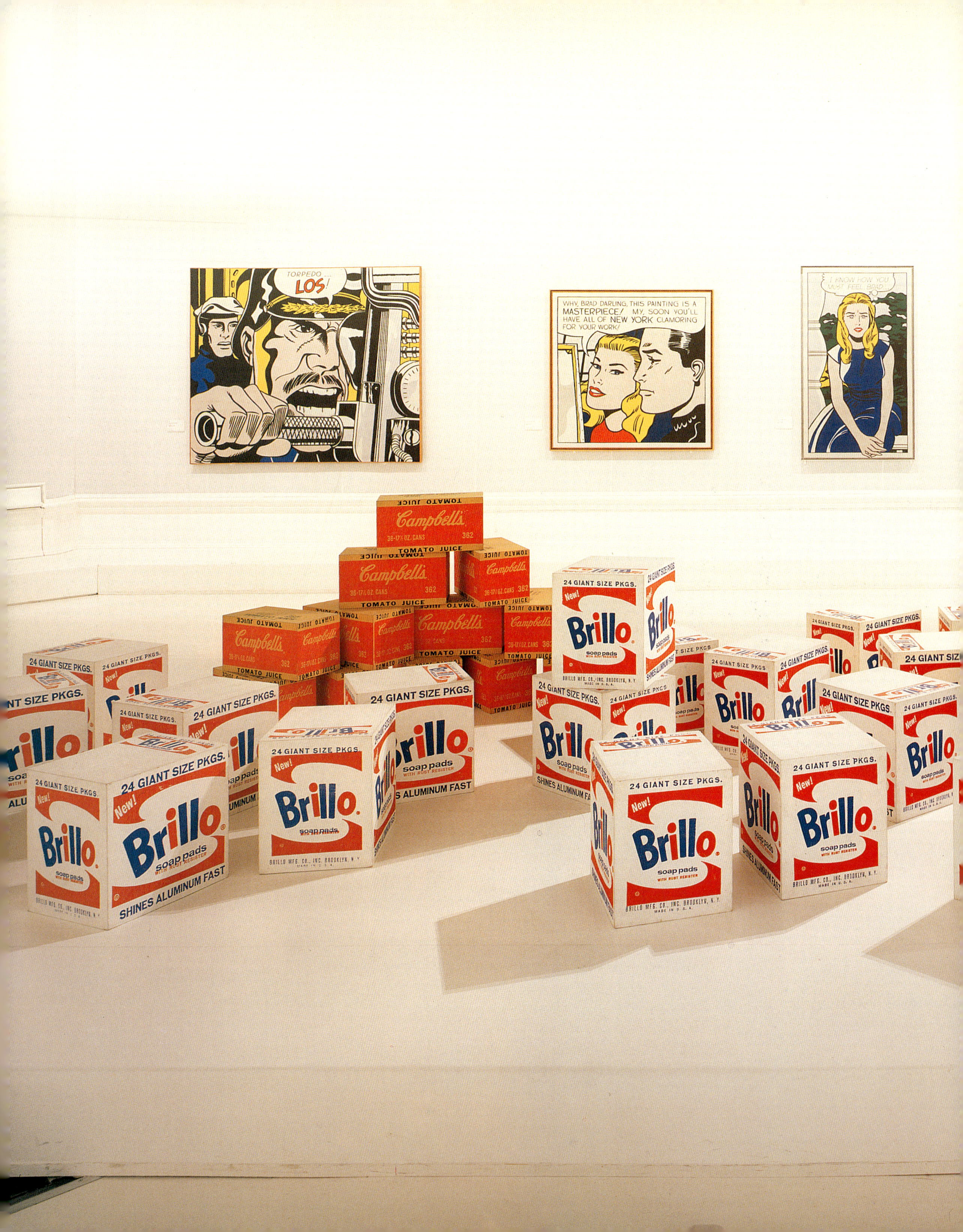
TORPEDO...
LOS!
WHY, BRAD DARLING, THIS PAINTING IS A MASTERPIECE! MY, SOON YOU'LL HAVE ALL OF NEW YORK CLAMORING FOR YOUR WORK!
I KNOW HOW YOU MUST FEEL BRAD...
TOMATO JUICE
Campbell's
36-17½ OZ. CANS 362
24 GIANT SIZE PKGS.
New!
Brillo
soap pads
WITH RUST RESISTER
SHINES ALUMINUM FAST
BRILLO MFG. CO., INC. BROOKLYN, N.Y.
MADE IN U.S.A.

An Art & Design Profile

Edited by Andreas C Papadakis

POP ART

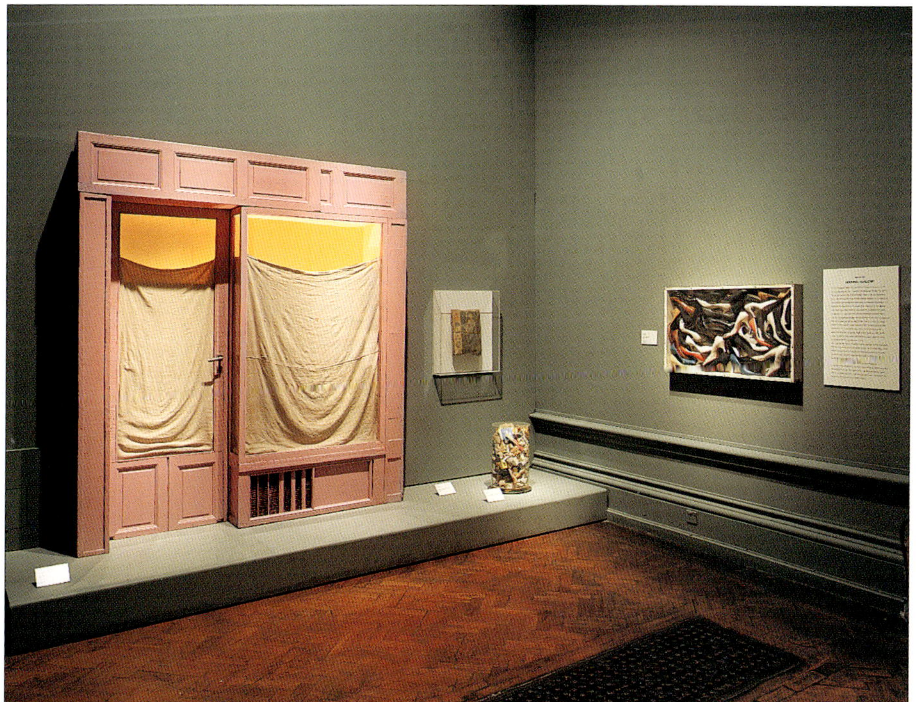

The Pop Art Show, Royal Academy, London, ABOVE: (left to right) Christo, Store Front, *1964;* Wrapped Magazines (Revues empaquetées), *1962; Arman,* Jim Dine's Dustbin (Poubelle), *1961;* Madison Avenue, *1962; OPPOSITE: (left to right), Roy Lichtenstein,* Torpedo . . . los!, *1963;* Masterpiece, *1962;* I Know . . . Brad, *1963; Andy Warhol,* Boxes, *1964 (photos Stephen White)*

ACADEMY EDITIONS • LONDON

Acknowledgements

This issue takes its theme from the 'POP ART SHOW'
at the Royal Academy of Arts London

Including interviews from the Pop Art Symposium organised by the Royal Academy of Arts and the Serpentine Gallery, which took place at the Royal Geographic Society, London on 12 September 1991, this issue celebrates the occurence of two major exhibitions, 'The Pop Art Show' at the Royal Academy, London (13 September-15 December 1991) and the exhibition 'Objects for the Ideal Home: The Legacy of Pop Art' at the Serpentine Gallery, London (11 September-20 October 1991). We are especially grateful to MaryAnne Stevens and Sara Gordon of the Royal Academy and Andrea Schlieker and Julia Little of the Serpentine Gallery for their help in compiling this issue and for permission to publish the specially commissioned installation shots by Stephen White. Thanks are also due to the National Sound Archive and the participants for allowing us to publish edited transcripts. The organisers of the Symposium would like to acknowledge the financial support of Lufthansa in arranging the visit of Jeff Koons.

We are grateful to the following artists, museums, galleries and publishers for providing us with material and assistance: *Back Cover*: Serpentine Gallery, London; *Inside Front Cover and Inside Back Cover*: Claes Oldenburg and Coosje van Bruggen, photo Pace Gallery; *Half-Title*: Apple Corps Ltd; **Introduction pp6-7**: *p6* Serpentine Gallery; **Rosenquist Interview pp8-13**: *p13* Museum of Contemporary Art, Los Angeles, Panza Collection; **Segal Interview pp14-19**: *p19* Virginia Museum of Fine Arts, gift of Sydney and Frances Lewis; **Jones Interview pp20-25**: material supplied by the artist; **Hamilton Interview pp26-37**: *p26* Kunsthalle Tübingen, Professor Dr Georg Zundel Collection; *p28* private collection; *p31* Museum Ludwig, Ludwig Donation, Cologne, *p30* private collection; **A Bridge Between Two Shows pp34-37**: Sonnabend Gallery, New York; **Koons Interview pp38-47**: material courtesy the artist and Sonnabend Gallery, New York, *p38* photo provided by Andreas Papadakis; **General Discussion pp48-61**: *p61* Waddington Galleries, London; **Pop Art in Britain pp62-73**: *p73* Waddington Galleries, London; **Moderne Kunst: European Pop pp74-81**: text and accompanying illustrations were reproduced from *Pop Art – A Continuing History*, Thames & Hudson, London, 1990, by permission of the publisher and Marco Livingstone, *p74* image and quote from the exhibition catalogue, *Gerhard Richter*, Tate Gallery Publications, London, 1991; **Christo pp82-89:** material courtesy the artist, photos by Wolfgang and Sylvia Volz; **Objects for the Ideal Home pp90-96:** text and accompanying illustrations were reproduced from the exhibition catalogue *Objects for the Ideal Home: The Legacy of Pop Art*, by permission of the Serpentine Gallery and Marco Livingstone, *p90* photo courtesy the Lisson Gallery.

EDITOR
Dr Andreas C Papadakis

EDITORIAL OFFICES: 42 LEINSTER GARDENS LONDON W2 3AN TELEPHONE: 071-402 2141
EDITORIAL TEAM: Nicola Hodges, Lucy Baxter, Vivian Constantinopoulos
DESIGN TEAM: Andrea Bettella, Mario Bettella, Owen Thomas, Sharon Anthony
ADVERTISING: Sheila de Vallée SUBSCRIPTIONS MANAGER: Mira Joka

First published in Great Britain in 1992 by *Art & Design*
an imprint of the
ACADEMY GROUP LTD, 7 HOLLAND STREET, LONDON W8 4NA
ISBN: 1 85490 134 6 (UK)

Art & Design Profile 24 is published as part of *Art & Design* Vol 6 11/12 90
Published in the United States of America by
ST MARTIN'S PRESS, 175 FIFTH AVENUE, NEW YORK 10010
ISBN: 0-312-07898-6 (USA)

Printed and bound in Singapore

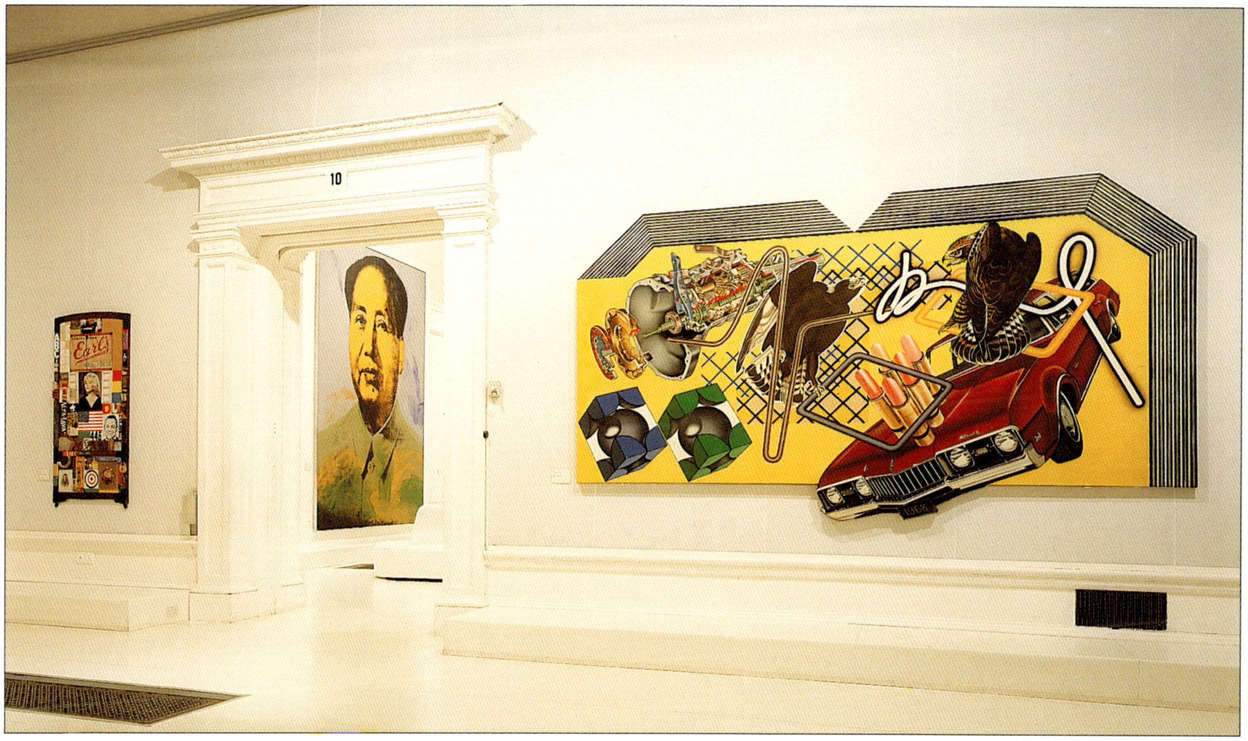

The Pop Art Show, Royal Academy, London, (left to right) Peter Blake, H.O.M.A.G.E. – JJ MM RR KS, 1991; Andy Warhol, Mao, *1973; Peter Phillips,* Random Illusion, No 6, *1969 (photo Stephen White)*

Contents

Subscription rates for 1991 (including p&p): Annual Rate: UK only £39.50, Europe £45.00, Overseas US$75.00 or UK sterling equiv. Student rates: UK only £35.00, Europe £39.50, Overseas US$65.00 or UK sterling equiv. Combined subscription with *AD*: UK only £75.00, Europe £85.00, Overseas US$135.00 or UK sterling equiv. Special student combined subscription: UK only $65.00, Europe £79.50, Overseas US$120.00 or UK sterling equiv. Individual double issues £7.95/US$14.95. Plus £1.00/US$3.00 per issue ordered for p&p. Printed in Singapore. [ISSN: 0267-3991]

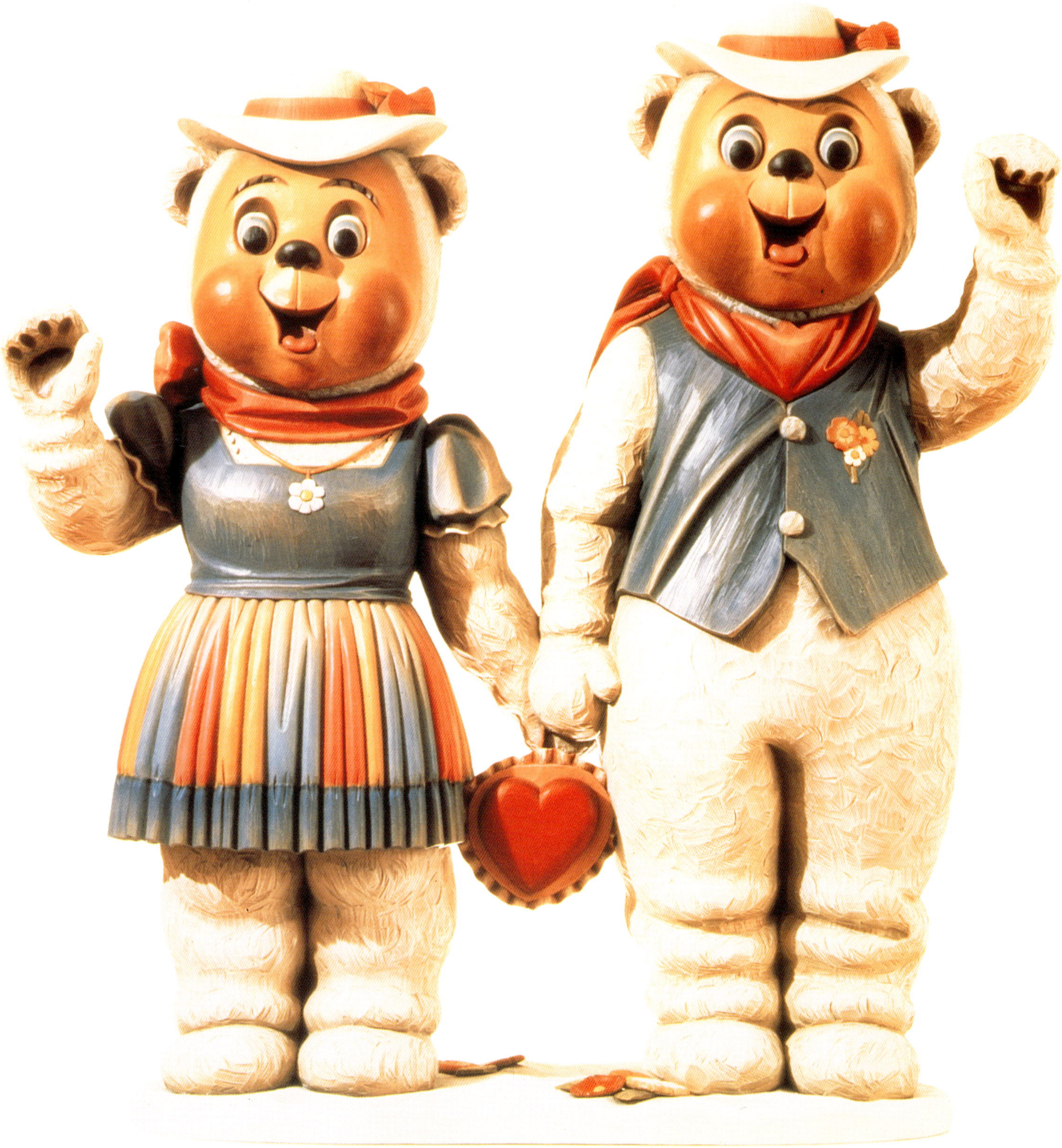

MARYANNE STEVENS
AN INTRODUCTION TO THE POP ART SYMPOSIUM

Jeff Koons, Winter Bears, *1988, polychrome wood, 122x112x39cm, from 'Objects for the Ideal Home: The Legacy of Pop Art', Serpentine Gallery, London*

Pop art from its inception provided problems of definition. As early as 1962 Henry Geldzahler recognised that the term must necessarily provide a broad umbrella under which a more or less identifiable group of artists might shelter. Alternatively, the term 'Neo-Realism' has been favoured, especially in a European context where the roots of much of this particular form of figurative art of the 1950s and 1960s lie in that quintessentially European mode of artistic expression, Dada. It was with this second definition in mind that it was decided to explore the common ground between the Pop Art Show, which opened at the Royal Academy in September 1991, and the exhibition exploring a younger generation's reaction to, or continuation of, the ideas of Pop figuration, at the Serpentine Gallery entitled 'Objects for the Ideal Home: The Legacy of Pop Art'.

This obvious conjunction of two exhibitions, which opened within one day of each other, encouraged the idea of mounting a one-day symposium, in which artists both of the 1960s and of the 1980s-1990s might participate, not with a series of formal papers but within a more informal format in which they would be interviewed by a leading critic. Given the Anglo-American thrust of the Royal Academy's show, the availability of major representative artists in London and their willingness to participate, James Rosenquist and George Segal were invited from the American side, and Allen Jones and Richard Hamilton from the British. For the younger generation, Ashley Bickerton and Jeff Koons accepted the invitations to contribute. The interviewers, six leading critics and art historians – five British and one American – were selected under the guidance of Marco Livingstone, the leading scholar on both the Royal Academy and Serpentine exhibitions. Finally, to provide a historical bridge between the two generations of Pop or Neo-Realist artists, the American critic Dan Cameron, author of one of the Royal Academy's catalogue essays, was invited to give a brief resumé of the background to the emergence of such artists as Bickerton and Koons during the 1980s.

The informal structure of the Pop Symposium, in which six artists were interviewed by six critics, could have produced a collection of nonsequential events. Under the informed guidance of each interviewer, followed by Marco Livingstone's expert handling of the final open discussion period, not only was a considerable amount of new historical material brought to light, but a sharper focus was given to definitional problems and the connections which might exist between the two generations of Pop/Neo-realist art.

JAMES ROSENQUIST

INTERVIEWED BY CONSTANCE GLENN

Constance Glenn: *I've heard Jim introduced in many ways and they're all very flattering. I think my favourite is still 'Ladies and gentlemen, the most famous artist ever born in the Happy Dragon Chinese Restaurant in Grand Forks, North Dakota,' which might lead us to talk about your background, growing up, painting billboards and commercial structures across the Midwest before you arrived in New York?*

James Rosenquist: Thank you. Thank you very much for the wonderful show and the recollection of all these artists and all these people. I feel very comfortable here. The hospital where I was born in North Dakota is now the Happy Dragon Chinese Restaurant, so I can't go back to where I came from.

Anyway, it's amazing to be asked over and over again in the past 30 years, 'What is Pop art?' and I'm surprised people are still asking. I look at the show and the beautiful thing is that the art works look the way they look in spite of photographs, in spite of art critics, in spite of all the aura that's around them. The truth is that one has to remember the era and the time. I see in the audience here George Segal, Bob Indiana, Allen Jones, Mel Ramos and maybe others. I remember them as young boys, but also the terrible temper that existed at the time the pictures were painted. I think of the tail-end of the 1950s when so-called Abstract Expressionism was at its height and I know how absurd I felt about what to do as an artist or even what kind of expression to make. And I remember some of us were very reactionary about not having any drips or splashes in our artwork.

I was a very reactionary art student; I used to know Bill de Kooning and Franz Kline and Barnett Newman and those fellows at the time when they were really starting to become known, and I thought this wasn't a profession at all, it was a private club. In New York there was the Friday Night Club, which seemed to be a very private gathering that saw art as a precious thing, quite separate from any kind of commercial art. Like a lot of people born with the ability to draw, or with artistic tendencies, my mother said, 'Why don't you try to make some money doing that?' I could draw naturally, ever since I was a little boy. I won a scholarship to the Minneapolis School of Art in 1948 and then in 1955 I won an out-of-town scholarship to the Art Students League on 57th Street in New York and that's what got me to Manhattan. I came to New York with $300 in my pocket. I had a room on 57th Street for $8.50 a week, I finally got an apartment for $30 a month and later a studio down in Coentie Slip for $45 a month. The reason I say all that is that now, for a youngster going to New York, it's extremely hard and expensive to exist. But the conditions of the era, the feelings of the time really had a great deal to do with the absurdity of trying to be an artist at that time. The reality in painting then seemed to be the shock of Jackson Pollock pouring paint out of an enamel can. So what else could one do beyond that? That was the great dilemma. Out of that came a lot of the work you see here today.

– *In the three 1961 paintings in the show, there are examples of what you've referred to as the strict close-up in* Hey, Let's Go for a Ride, *the juxtaposed elements that other people have called collage in* Look Alive *and what you call tri-focal vision in* I Love You With My Ford. *And you talk about these three kinds of vision as things that you've adapted from billboard painting. I thought that you might want to talk about Franco-American spaghetti red and some of these different types of billboard painting that you finally acknowledged in your art.*

OVERLEAF: The Pop Art Show, Royal Academy, London, (left to right) James Rosenquist, Look Alive (Blue Feet, Look Alive), *1961;* Hey, Let's Go for a Ride, *1961;* I Love You with My Ford, *1961 (photo Stephen White)*

In New York, I transferred into the International Sign Painters and Pictorial Painters Union Local 230, and I got a job in Brooklyn painting a Hebrew National Salami sign as my first job. It was very difficult because it looked like the Superman logo and I didn't know how to do it. I could paint pictures of anything but I didn't know how to letter very well. Finally, I graduated to Times Square and there I painted the Astor Victoria Theatre sign seven times and the Castro Convertible sign about seven times. When they weren't good enough the salesman would be there quickly saying, 'There isn't enough hops in that beer, the Arrow shirt collars are dirty, you gotta change it.' I thought, how do you paint more hops into the beer? So I changed the yellow slightly and they said that's fine, that passes. Same with the colour orange; I'd paint a big orange for Sunkist oranges and the next day I'd paint a big Early Times whiskey bottle that was the same orange, it was very peculiar. So colour became metaphors. When it was the wrong colour, I used to take it home in a can and make abstract paintings with it. I had dirty Arrow shirt tan, I had Franco-American spaghetti orange, I had all these wrong colours. I thought what a pun, making all these abstract paintings out of the wrong colours.

In about 1959-60, I quit. I got a studio down on Coentie Slip near where Bob Indiana was living, who I had run into over the years, and Ellsworth Kelly, Bob Rauschenberg, and a number of other people. They said there's this studio that's 45 bucks a month, which was terrific, really nothing. I didn't have any expenses, so I didn't have a care in the world. I knew a number of the so-called Beat generation, people who didn't care about anything anyway. I was also interested in French existentialism and in non-objective painting, where one is only interested in pure colour and pure form, and the idea of not harking back to the feeling of earlier art. I thought that I could make a new kind of picture in which fragments would be set in space so that the closest piece of fragment would be recognised last, and I could develop some mystery in my art. They were all generic things, they weren't really brand names or anything like that. The reason was that I wanted to appeal to the viewer. I wanted the previous generation of artists – the Friday Night Club – to claim it as art. The group that I became affiliated with later was much cooler. It was up to someone else to call it art, they didn't demand it.

– *You made a comparison the other day with American Pop art and your perception of British and Continental Pop art in terms of the materials available to all of you to make art from.*

I was born in the United States and grew up there in the 30s, 40s and 50s, and I lived with pastel coloured toilets and bath tubs and used to see Sugar Ray Robinson's pink Cadillac convertible in Harlem, where I used to work, and I was surrounded by all the exterior ambience of colour that existed in the United States. My first show in Paris was in 1964. I went there and looked around and I had a hard time finding junk or scrap to make a collage in France. Even art materials were pretty difficult to get in post-war France. I remember young French artists sitting around at Café Flore developing their art but not really being able to practise it.

– *You said you thought a lot of this punchy quality that is sometimes called garish in American Pop art came out of the quality of the media available to you. For years you learned to hide your sources from*

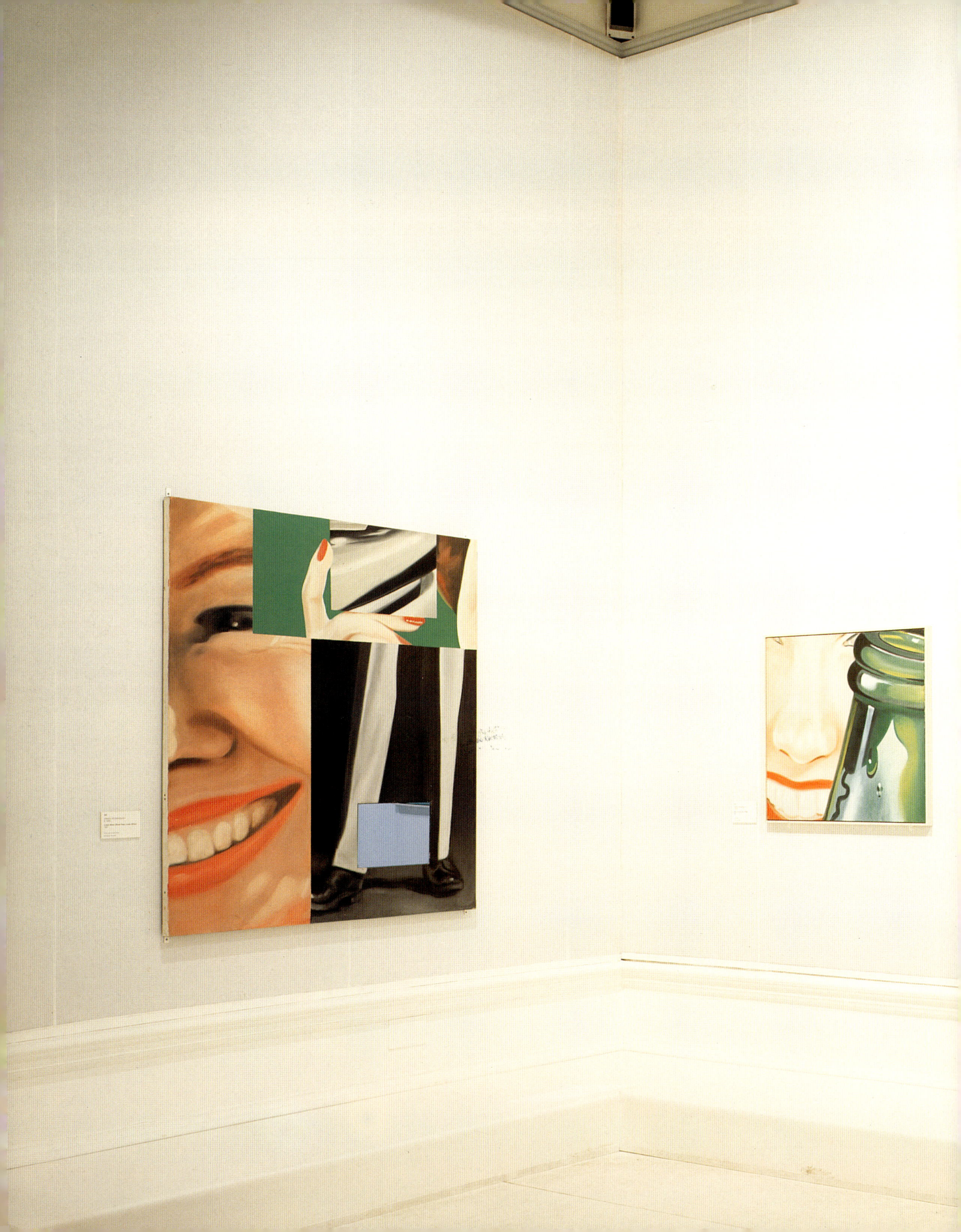

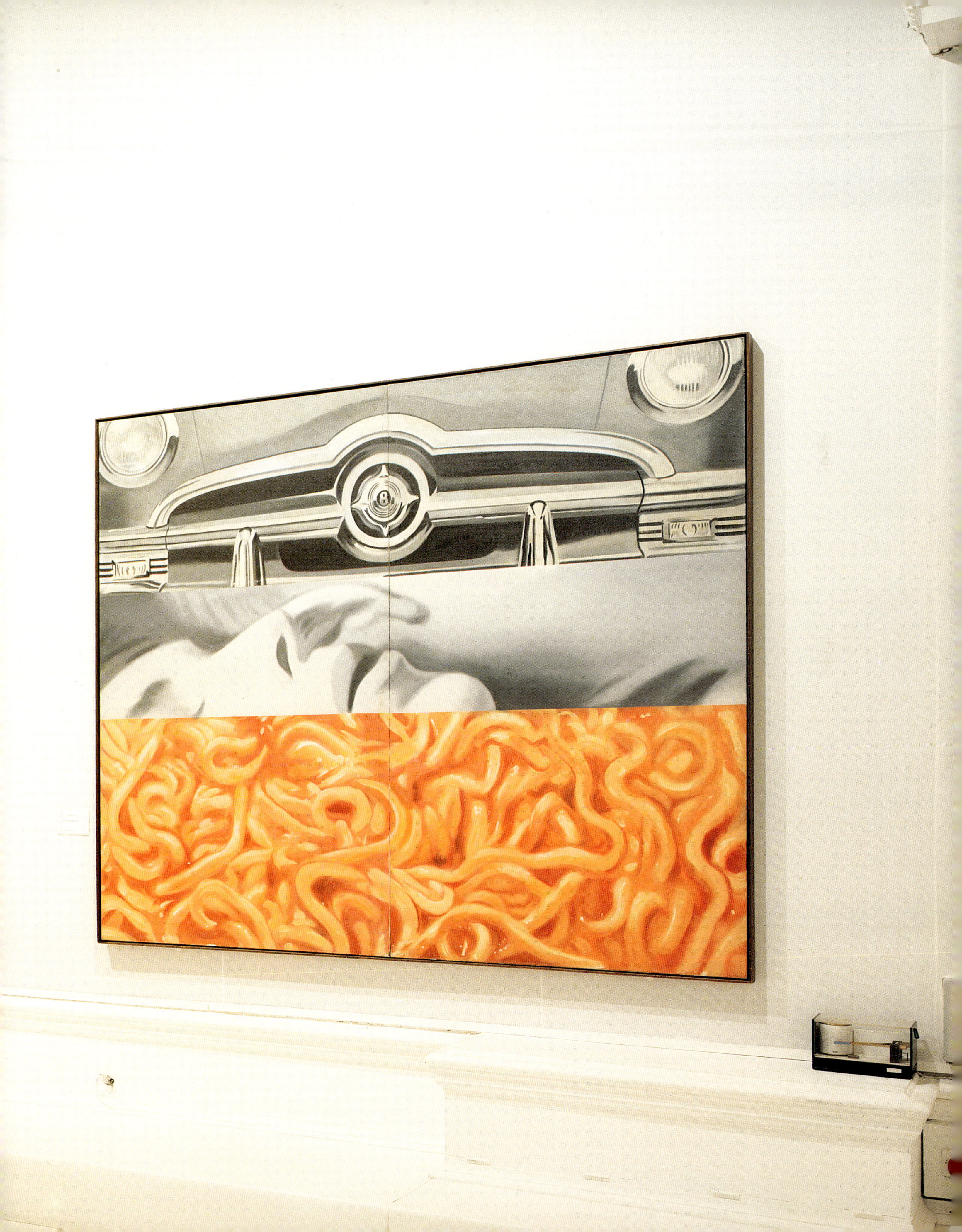

the sign painters so they wouldn't copy what you were doing and now, after 30 years, you're finally going to publish some of the sources that you used from the popular media.

I never used to show my painting sketches or how I developed them, but now I think that it probably doesn't matter.

– *What about your interest in Duchamp, whom you used to know?*

I met him a few times and had conversations with him, but I didn't know him that well. I met him at Yvonne Thomas' the first time and I brought him a sunflower fly-swatter and a Mona Lisa New York button because Mona Lisa had visited New York. He loved them. He sat around and swatted imaginary flies and put on his big button and he was very pleasant. I remember most young art students in New York thought Marcel Duchamp was very unapproachable, but he was actually very social and very friendly.

– *You were working on the largest scale of any of your contemporaries in 1961, yet the pictures that seemed so big in 1961 look quite small next to* Star Thief. *How big is big for you, Jim?*

It was really not a matter of bigness. The point was to make things cooler and more impersonal. In my first pictures, all the imagery was larger than life and that simply came from painting large things in Times Square, where I'd check out my work from two blocks away and I'd notice that the top of the bottle of Coke I was drinking was the same size as the one two blocks away and the immediate recognition of time changed. I had the notion that I'd like to bring these experiences inside a room and I tried to do that several times. There are a lot of things I've never done. Some young students think that they are at an endpoint and that everything's been done, but it certainly hasn't – a tremendous number of things are still exciting.

– *You began to use a cross-hatching technique, particularly since living in Florida. Some critics have called them slashes and seen them as vicious, assaultive to women, dangerous looking, etc.*

Many artists have juxtaposed one form with another in looking for new space in a picture plane. I thought why couldn't I use just enough of a suggestion of one image, and put on top another image like a Venetian blind so that they became like shards of information, so that the combination of those two ideas might produce another idea. The part about the women really had to do with seeing wild animals down in Florida and then seeing women in Manhattan.

– *How do those relate?*

Seeing men and women being very sophisticated on Madison Avenue or in London, and then seeing people looking very natural in Florida; seeing fingernails, nostrils, ears on a person and then seeing them on a wild animal . . . So I started doing paintings about reincarnation or habitats in animals and people all mixed up with flowers and cacti, or people with machinery. The question that fascinated me was, how do young people want to live in the future? A few years ago, a high-tech apartment was very popular, but do people want to live in that environment or would they prefer to live like a lamb in the meadow? That still remains to be seen.

– *Talking in terms of shards brings us up to date. Do you want to say anything about* Time Dust, *both the print you're working on and your concept or your feelings about* Time Dust*?*

Liv Ullman asked me what I was going to do next, and I said I'm going to do the persistence of electrical nymphs in space. And she said, 'Oh, what is that about?' and I said, 'That's the sound of all the souls after the earth blows up,' and she goes, 'Oh, yeah.' I couldn't faze her at all, she's been living with Ingmar Bergman too long.

I personally think that it's very interesting to get a reaction by doing something about a capitalist economy, about society. Painting a Coke bottle or something that one can recognise, you can certainly get an immediate reaction but I think that I used those generic items to produce a new pictorial idea. I did a series of quite large mixed-media prints called *Welcome to the Water Planet.* It was an idea of what new frontiers are available to a young person. They might think of going to Alaska, LA, Hawaii, Australia; or maybe space is the place to go, though it's a little pricey yet. The study available to young people could be time, things having to do with ecology, and a number of other things in these prints that I did. One title of one print was *Where the Water Goes* – and where do things go after you throw them away? That's curious.

– *People ask you fairly often if your art is political or socially/ecologically concerned. You told me that politics are there, you either have to use them or throw them away. Did you use them or did you throw them away?*

Well, for me the idea to get up off the chair to try to make a picture could be almost anything; it may be a number of ideas. When the pictures are seen later, art critics and viewers will claim that it means a certain thing, but there may be quite a bit more to it than that.

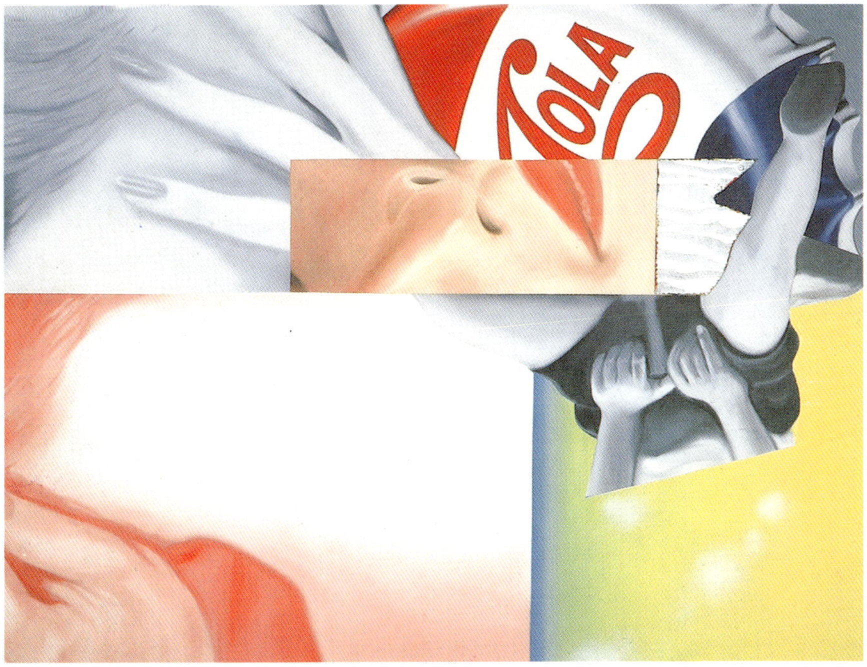

James Rosenquist, Vestigial Appendage, *1962, oil, 183x237cm*

GEORGE SEGAL
INTERVIEWED BY ANDREW GRAHAM-DIXON

Andrew Graham-Dixon: *Do you think you're a Pop artist? How do you feel when people say, 'There's George Segal the Pop artist?' Or maybe they don't.*

George Segal: That depends on your definition of Pop art. I feel like we're all characters in the Japanese movie *Rashomon* today. I had a strange time last night looking at the show. The joy and delight of art critics is practising critical ranking; you're number one, two, three or 29. My overwhelming reaction last night was, I know everybody or almost everybody. I certainly know all the Americans, and my relationship to them, to their ideas and my mental life for the past 30 years has very little to do with the show, the catalogue and all the critical talk.

– *Do you actually feel as if your work doesn't belong there? Do you feel like an outsider?*

No, absolutely not. I'll give you a worm's-eye view. When I was an art student I was overwhelmed by the look of Abstract Expressionist painting, which was brand-new in New York. I wanted to become a fine artist, and my father said, 'You bum! You'll never make a living at it, and I can't support you.' That loving paternal injunction is overwhelming.

I was at an art school, trying to learn how to make myself into an art teacher and sneaking in fine art in a clandestine way. I saw an exhibition of what I later discovered to be student derivative imitation Abstract Expressionism being done at New York University and I instantly switched, I fell in love with it. My direct teachers were overwhelming father figures: Tony Smith was one, Baziotes was another. Smith used to walk down the halls with Rothko paintings under his arm, showing us what the new work looked like and inviting me to go to club meetings. I started to try to paint Abstract Expressionist. There was this terrible pressure on young artists to jump on the bandwagon of the history of art with this new thing. I was told to get a big canvas and a five-inch housepainter's brush and to use black and white. I said, 'What do I paint?'

I was totally split. I loved the look of the paint. This was NYU, Washington Square, right after the war. Everybody was in art school because they had a GI bill paying tuition. New York City was full of refugee great European artists and there was an excitement in the air, there was this competitive challenge; the Americans were chauvinistically swaggering, seeing the suffering of these European exiles in a totally unfamiliar city. We thought they were demi-gods because we had seen reproductions of the stupendous School of Paris work. We were going to challenge this supremacy in the same way that as young art students (forgive me for being peripheral, I'm getting excited about that time) we had discovered jazz and we had the nerve to go up to Harlem because we were young and we could physically take care of ourselves and we would listen to the new jazz by black musicians.

Faced with Abstract Expressionism, I thought it was marvellous: they were anti-materialist, they sounded like New York cab drivers and they talked James Joyce. Tony Smith would show us Cubist paintings by Picasso and say, 'What are the connections between James Joyce and these Cubist paintings?' The toughness, the brashness, the harshness of New York was balanced by this last refuge of idealism. You couldn't expect to make money at it, you were stupid if you did. If you wanted to learn about and practise fine art no matter what the form, you had to find some other way to support yourself. That was bluntly it.

So in that atmosphere, I quarrelled. I loved Tony Smith and Baziotes but I quarrelled with them. They left me no room to grapple with the world I could see and touch with my hand. Everything they were talking about was staggeringly admirable – pure form, the expressiveness of the paint, of the colour, of the history of art and the enormous possibilities for new art. I floundered around. I graduated, and that entitled me to teach art though I knew nothing about it. I went home, where my father had a chicken farm across the road, and I built a chicken farm too. This is the stock joke that is comparable to James Rosenquist painting billboards; I became a chicken farmer.

I met Allan Kaprow and he introduced me not only literally to Rauschenberg, Johns, John Cage and Merce Cunningham, but also to this world of ideas. Kaprow was a strange hybrid; he was teaching art history, he published articles regularly in *Art News* about the new art, and it took me ten years to discover that he was a master of esoteric mystery because he knew what Futurism looked like, which I had never heard of at the time. He knew about Neo-Dada and the Dada-Surrealist movement, and he somehow knew intimately what happened at the Café Ball in Zurich. He knew about concrete poetry and things like that. Finally he took me to a Cage class.

– *When did you meet Kaprow?*

I met Kaprow in 53. I graduated from NYU, a licensed art teacher, and started building my chicken farm. He got a job and happened to move in down the road, and some mutual friend introduced us; we were going to invent the New Brunswick School of painting in New Brunswick, New Jersey. I became a member of the cooperative gallery that Kaprow belonged to. All those people had been students of Hans Hofmann, I was the only exception. They included Yosten Kevitch who is a child of David Smith, working with street garbage. Besides Kaprow my other buddy was Jan Muller, who was a refugee from Germany. His father had been a socialist and he was a figurative painter of scenes from Shakespeare. Myron Stout did black-and-white abstract paintings that he called the seed pods of the gods, which were figurative expressionism via Van Gogh. So New York was a wallowing goulash of every kind of painting that was an echo of Abstract Expressionism or a reaction against it.

– *Would you say that there was one Pop art, if we accept the label for a minute? Looking at the American artists in this exhibition, was there a strong sense of community among you or was it more that there were mini-communities within that; I mean, were you ever particularly close with, let's say, Claes Oldenburg or Roy Lichtenstein?*

Yes. I think we all gravitated towards each other. I think the common glue was dissatisfaction with Abstract Expressionism. Not, strangely enough, with the look of it. The critic Clement Greenberg had made a mighty pronouncement that the history of 20th-century art was an implacable march toward abstraction and there was this rigorous exorcism of everything figurative in art.

I thought that was laughable and I was attracted to artists my own age who also objected to that

OVERLEAF: The Pop Art Show, Royal Academy, London, (left to right) George Segal, Woman Standing in a Bathtub, *1964;* Artist in His Loft, *1969; Robert Indiana,* American Gas Works, *1962;* Zig, *1960 (photo Stephen White)*

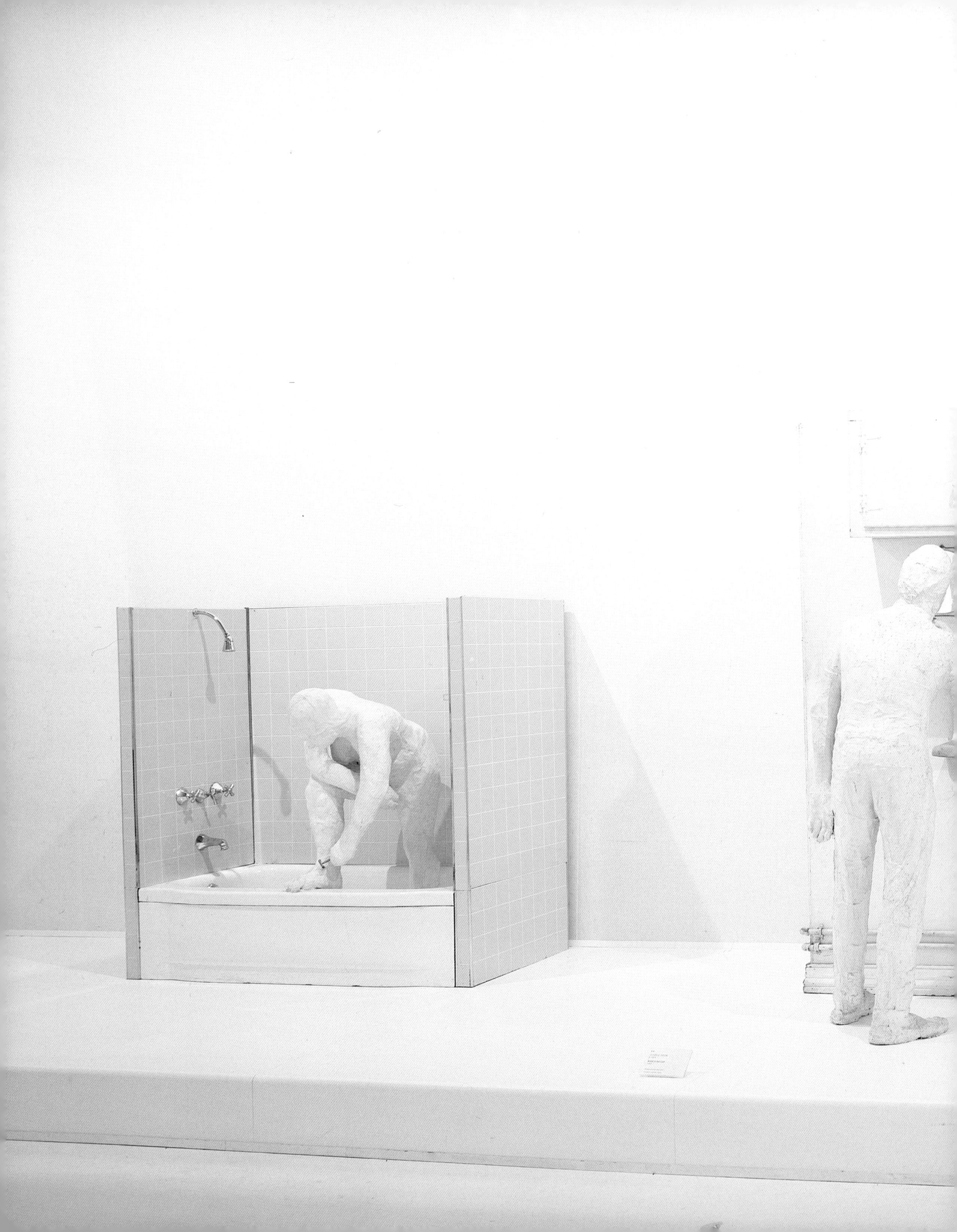

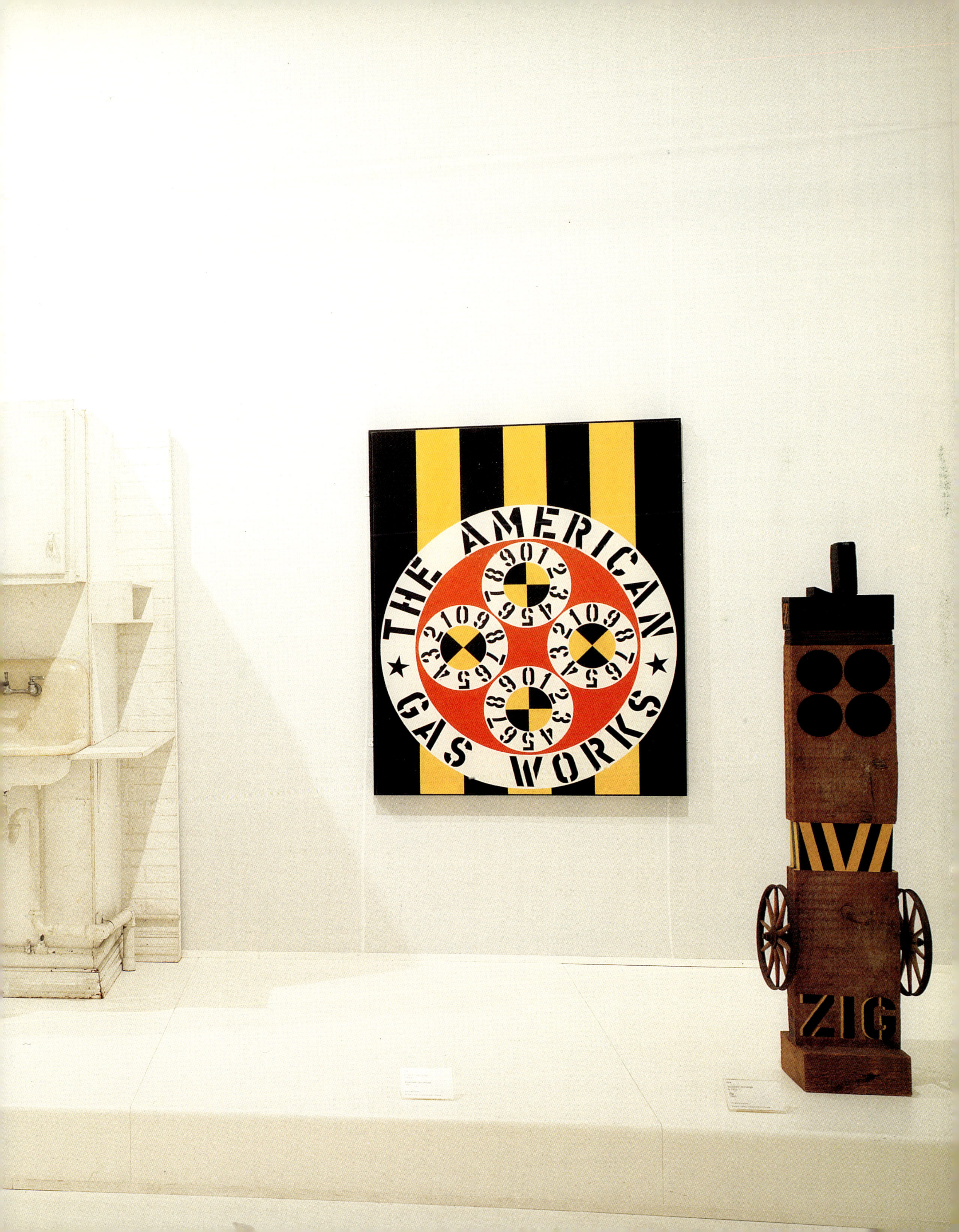
THE AMERICAN
GAS WORKS
ZIG

ordered scenario. Yes, I knew Lichtenstein, Oldenburg, Dine, Kaprow; I knew all the people in the Fluxus movement. There was a feeling of community in those early years; we all shared a certain mental life. I once loaned my farm to Kaprow, who organised six international happenings. Vostell smashed and destroyed a TV set on my chicken farm. A student of Kaprow scavenged the tubes the next morning, which I thought was very good. Kaprow did a happening. He had an army of people armed with twigs ripped out of the woods – I guess it's Burnham Wood – and he asked me to order a bulldozer in which he was going to oppose this army. I censored his artwork. I told him, 'You never drove a bulldozer before, suppose you slip and kill somebody?' He said, 'Oh, no.' I said, 'Oh, well, I'm censoring your artwork.' It's things like that, but that's practical nonsense.

– *You never actually made happenings yourself, did you? But there's a sense of theatre present in your work. Do you think there's any relationship there?*

No, Kaprow did a lot of work on the happenings; he made a whole string of them with a long list of artists: Oldenburg, Dine, Red Grooms, Bob Whitman all made happenings. Each time, Kaprow would publish a new article and envelope the artist's personal statement into his grand theory, and they used to get very mad at him. But all this was part of the building of a new art movement. I objected to the happenings purely in terms of their ephemeral form. I loved the idea of being able to enter a physical space and walk around it and for it to be punctuated by severe, austere forms that were fragments of the real world. For me, it was literal Cubism – I could walk around it and see it from different points of view. But I was more introspective; I wanted to enter it over and over again and I objected to writing a happening that was performed six times and then existed only as a single typewritten sheet of instructions. I was hungry to make forms with my own hands.

That was my quarrel with Kaprow – I was always quarrelling with somebody, I don't know why, maybe that is the whole point – it became so totally cerebral; the expression of your head depended on it being acted out, and the delicate nuances changed from week to week. I thought Kaprow was wiping out the history of art, which has to do primarily with the pleasure of making your own forms, if there's any validity to that. I quarrelled with the Abstract Expressionists because they wanted me to leave out the real world. They spoke just like the Humanists; they had all kinds of noble intentions except everything was couched in pure colour, pure form, thick or thin or marvellous paint. I used Duchamp's ideas as a precedence or justification of the found object, which is anonymous; nobody knows who made it. It is mass-produced in a factory system and it is poignant and full of associations. In spite of itself, a found object is extraordinarily expressive.

I've never pretended to be cool, witty, detached or ironic. I have great admiration for Lichtenstein, who is a close personal friend. The fact that he's cooler than I makes no difference but I am a prisoner of my own temperament and I can't apologise for dealing with expressive feeling.

– *You talk about found objects, but in, say,* Woman Standing in a Bathtub, *you chose the object, it's not just something that you happened upon. There's a difference with Duchamp, isn't there?*

Duchamp wrote that in one of my catalogues. Sidney Janis asked him to write a preface to my catalogue, and he came up with a single hand-written sentence: 'With Segal, it's not the found object it's the chosen object.'

– Did you know Duchamp?

Yes, I met him late on, I felt he was unapproachable. I discovered his fragility and vulnerability and Rosenquist was quite accurate in how he characterised Marcel. I think Marcel's grandness lies in the strength of his ideas. I'd say the same about Cage. Cage is a role model, exemplary life, the consummate philosopher, cool and unflappable; I don't believe that for a second. I don't believe the coolness propaganda at all.

– Was Cage an influential figure for you? Was he or is he a friend of yours?

Hard to define friend; we know each other, we've seen each other for years and I've been warm with Cage and Cunningham for a long time. We meet at these public occasions.

– Did you ever go to a Cage performance say in the 60s and think, yeah, he's interested in what I'm interested in, there's a sense of contact, there's a sense of community.

Absolutely. I did go to an original performance. David Tudor performed *Four Minutes, Thirty-two Seconds of Silence*. Tudor came in very fussily like a pretentious concert pianist and he sat down and he moved his elbows and he arranged things and then nothing happened. Finally people caught on and they started to shuffle and you could hear traffic noise coming in from the window and lights were blinking. I became intensely aware of the space of the room and the quality of the sound because psychologically it was coitus interruptus. I was grinning from ear to ear and I was in an absolute state of delight because this was precisely like the poetry of the real world in contra-distinction to the rules, regulations, boundaries, restrictions, fences of Abstract Expressionist painting. It opened up the poetic possibilities of the real world. It's terrible to be a young painter, you're expected to re-invent the wheel. Every generation is supposed to number one, become personal, number two, invent a new grammar, a new way of saying it. You literally couldn't use Renaissance space, you would be sneered at, they would take your club membership away.

I'm supposed to be a Pop artist. I don't pretend to be witty, detached or ironic. I think I'm interested in something like a unified field theory. It has to do with preserving what's best in abstraction, which is the unquestioned power of pure composition to express what is unconscious. Unconscious, that means all those invisible feelings that are trapped inside our body that we all experience plus some evidence of this materialistic, miraculous, sometimes brutal real world outside our skin.

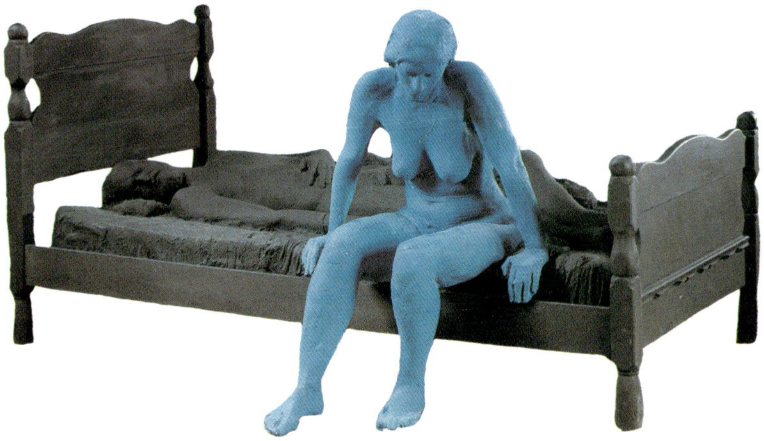

George Segal, Blue Girl on Black Bed, *1976, painted plaster, wood, 111x208x152cm*

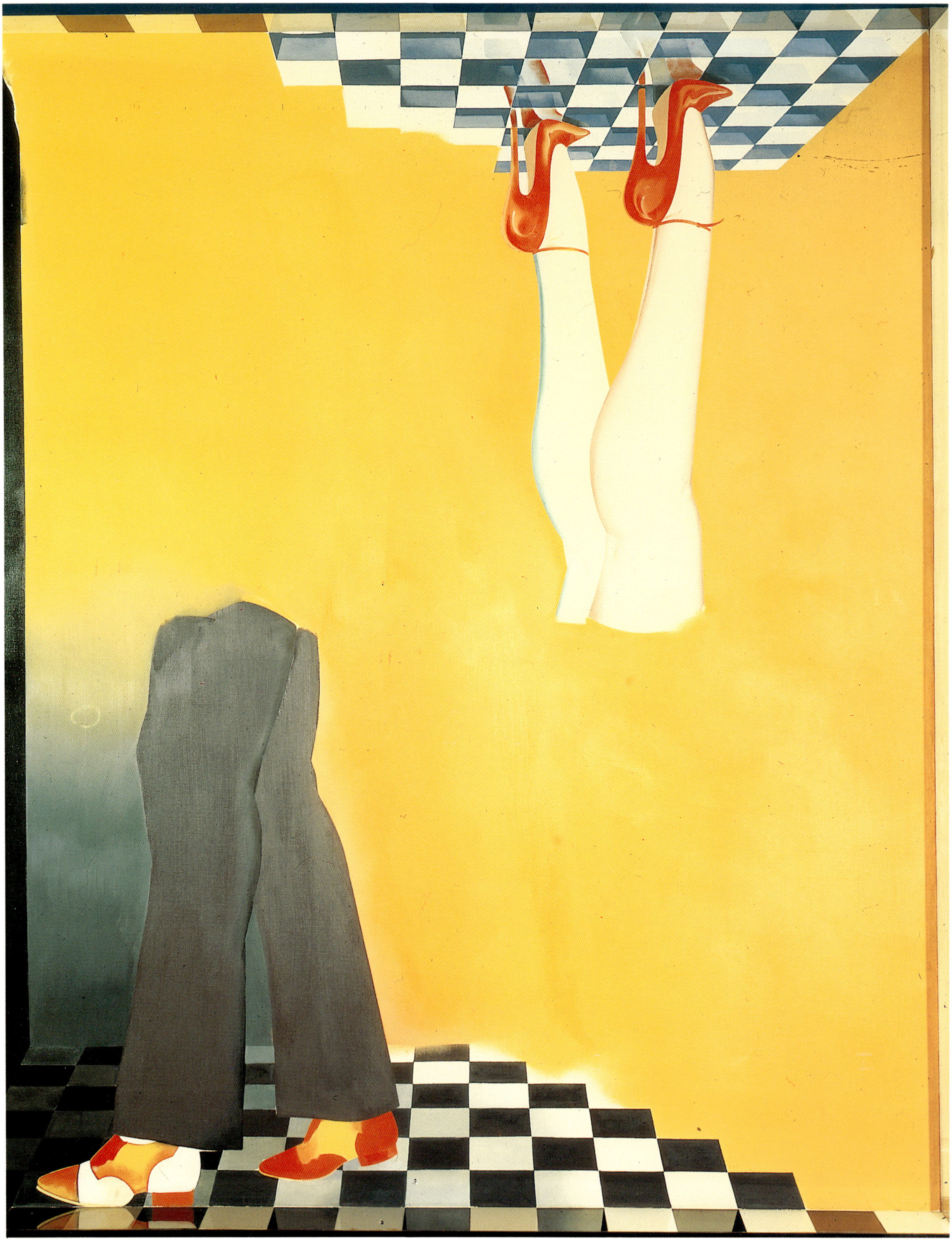

ALLEN JONES

INTERVIEWED BY MARCO LIVINGSTONE

Allen Jones, A Matter of Fact, *1967, oil*

Marco Livingstone: *I think if we had time for all 60 or so artists in the exhibition to talk for half an hour about their work, we would get 60 rather different stories about how it all happened and the importance of the movement in changing art over the last 30 years. There was an extraordinary sudden flowering of a British form of Pop art with very close connections among you. Could you explain this extraordinary coincidence that you, David Hockney, RB Kitaj, Derek Boshier, Peter Phillips came together and seemed to have, at least for two or three years, similar preoccupations and a similar way of re-invigorating art in this country.*

Allen Jones: We were all born around about the same time and went through the school system and happened to end up in the same place. Having listened to two fine painters from America, it is hard to convey how much more romantic and idealised their world seemed to us from our side of the Atlantic. What interests me is how much experience in fact we seemed to have had in common, despite these artists referring to a decade before. As young students at that time, we were up against Abstract Expressionism too, but exposed to the English version represented by a group of artists in an exhibition called 'Situation' mounted by Lawrence Alloway.

I always characterised the English artists as being people who had seen the American stuff in reproduction and didn't know that it actually had a very funky painterly surface. English abstract painting at that time was about formal presentation of shallow space, and was really informed by American painting.

I remember seeing a Pollock show at the Whitechapel with the artist Ken Kiff, when we were students. It was staggering to think that we had been to art school for five years and we walked into the Whitechapel and had no idea where this came from, what the rationale was, what the basis was for it.

– *What was the date of the Pollock show?*

I would have thought it was 1958.

– *That's before you went to the Royal College.*

Yes, that's right. All this happened just prior to the realisation and the ability to go to New York.

– *It's interesting that you should bring up New York because it seems to me that the problem one has with the label 'Pop' is that it encompasses so many different things that happened more or less simultaneously and that had very little relationship to each other. At the beginning, Peter Blake's first works came about very much through his own personal enthusiasm for the circus and wrestling and so on. And Jasper Johns' flags and Rauschenberg's combines were happening at the same time in*

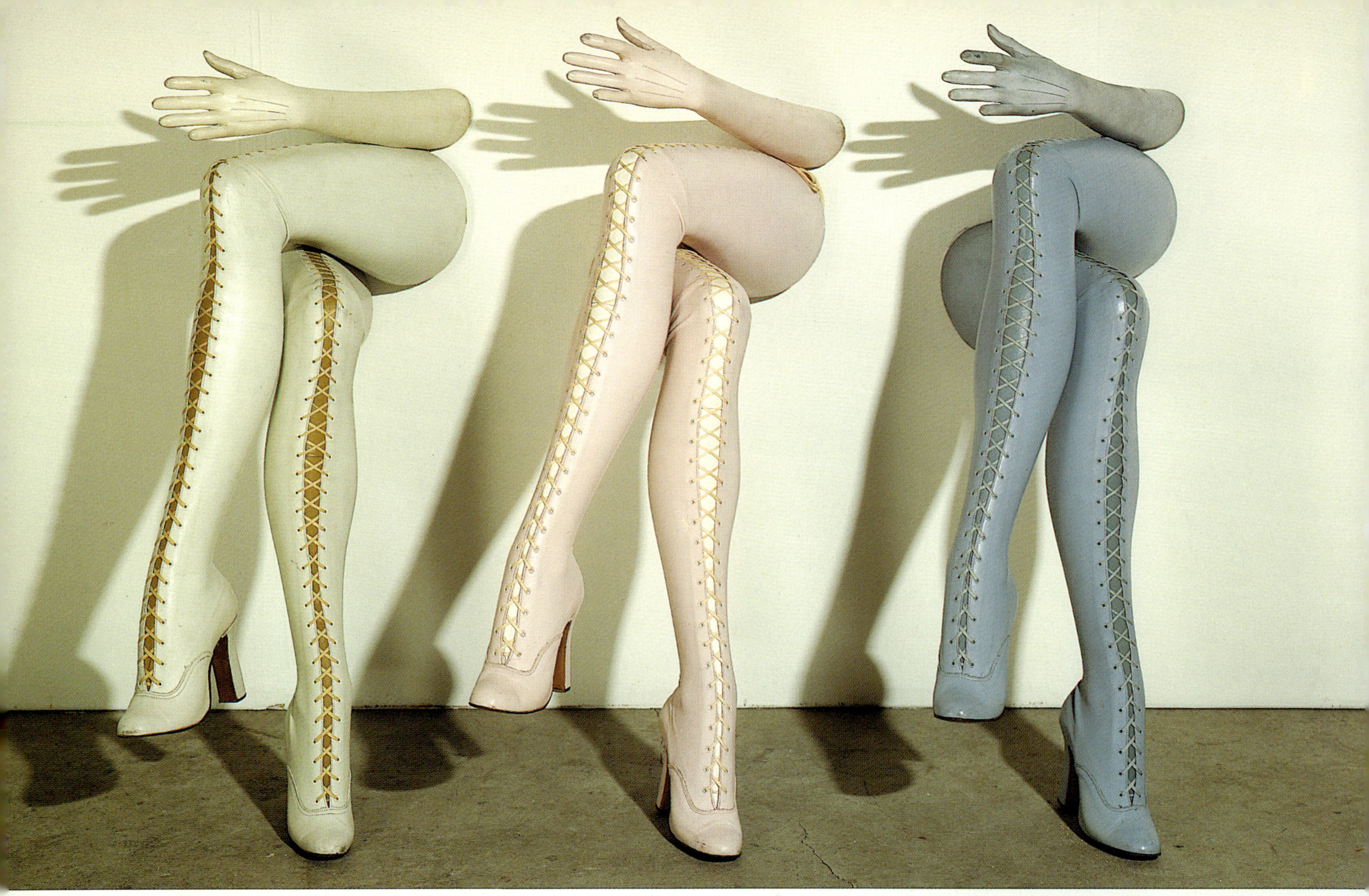

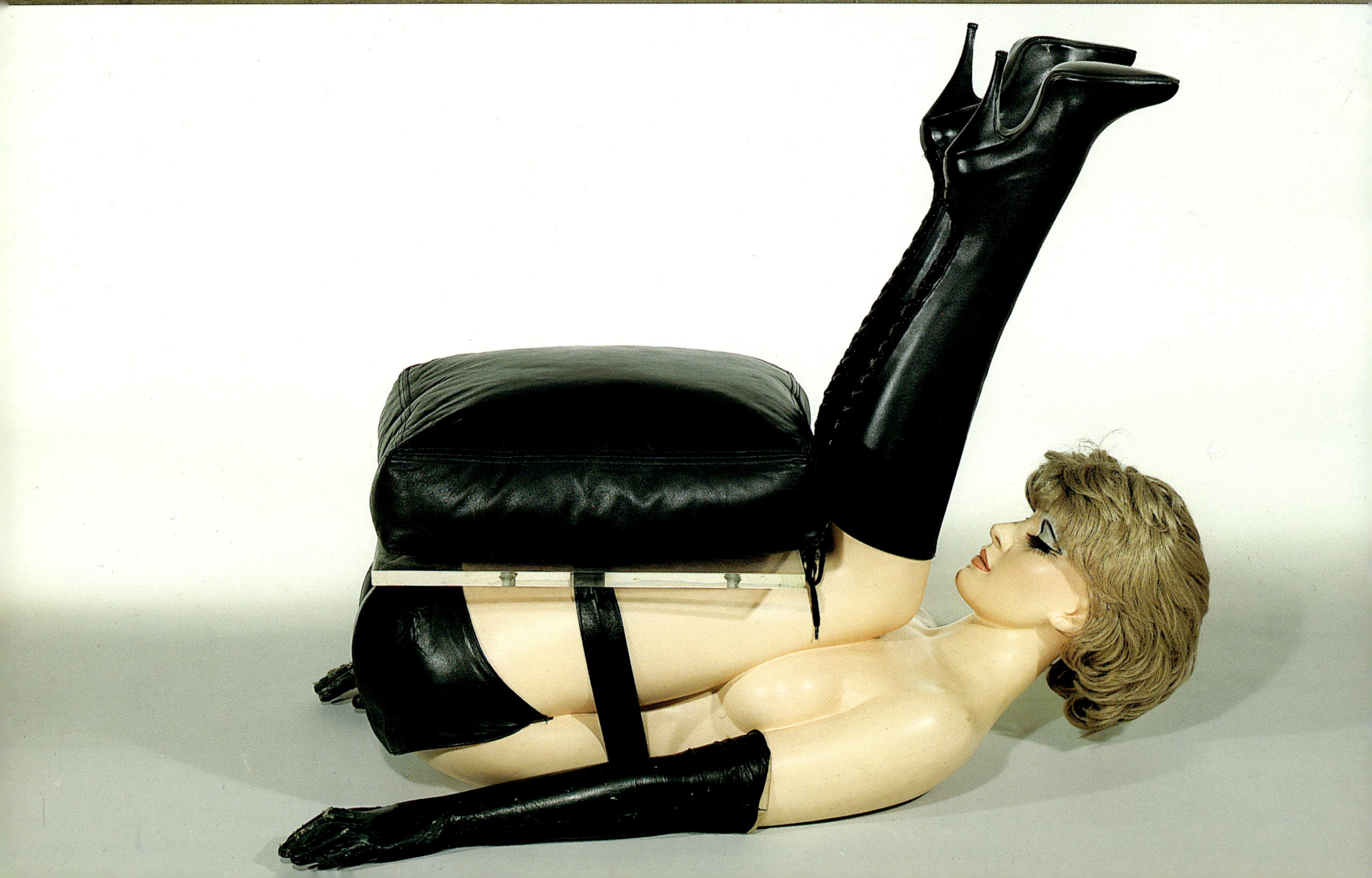

response to very different conditions. It seems to me that in New York your work took on board a lot of the issues in American work – the scale, for example, and that kind of boldness and immediacy. At what stage did you feel that it really became an issue of taking on board the American challenge?

Allen Jones, Secretary, *1972, legs sculpture*

Allen Jones, Chair, *1969, mixed media, edition of six, 77x100cm*

I still think that there is a very clear difference between the way that pictorial space is dealt with between American and European artists, in spite of the apparent imagery plundered from popular sources. I always feel when looking at a Lichtenstein in particular that I'm looking at a painting that's emblematic and heraldic; I think that attitude towards the surface is not shared by European artists. One of the points of going to New York of course was that one wanted to be able to see for oneself and realise that what seemed to be value judgements were simply cultural differences.

– *I think people often still see Pop art as an American movement and the English equivalent as in some way an off-shoot of it. But if you look at the chronology, when you did your painting* The Artist Thinks *in 1960 or* Thinking About Women *in 1961, both of which contain an allusion to a comic-strip think balloon, nothing was known about Lichtenstein or about Warhol's comic-strip paintings; they hadn't been seen here.*

Looking back on the earlier work, it was the work of a young man who was trying to ram the ideas and things that he wanted to paint through a kind of fine art grille, so that it came out looking like serious fine art; the presence of art history sits on those pictures. I think that it's a characteristic of young work generally, and that the process of maturity is realising that you have to go for it. There's risk involved, but that business of going straight for it and making the formal issue the product of the necessity of the painting as opposed to it being a language which you've learned and can perform in, is a difference which I see in the development of my work.

I suppose I do think Pop art is an American movement, I think that the tyranny of a linear view of history will sort of coagulate into another reality. That idea of who's doing what in Omaha and who's doing what in Düsseldorf is marginally interesting, but maybe you can draw some broad conclusions about the state of society at that time. Just as the progress of scientific knowledge would be radically different if everybody engaged in some form of investigation could read about everybody else who was doing the same thing in another country. It's staggering, the small percentage of information which even in this modern world is translated into a language which makes it meaningful to the two or three people in the world who are working in related fields. For me, what happened was that I responded to things in magazines and art programmes. I was in a student situation and suddenly realised that it was possible to represent people or images from everyday life. This notion of art history as a system of paring away and dumping has been mentioned earlier on. It seems to be an idiotic idea that it would no longer be possible for people to depict a tree. I would love to be able to depict a tree, I can't find or think of a formal way of doing it at the moment.

– *To what extent do you think the situation has changed since you were a student? Your group were all in your mid 20s when you produced the paintings that are on show here, and it was something very new in England for artists to reach a large public at such an early age. Now there's a feeling among artists that by the time they leave art school they have to be fully formed with their own aesthetic and a very clear image.*

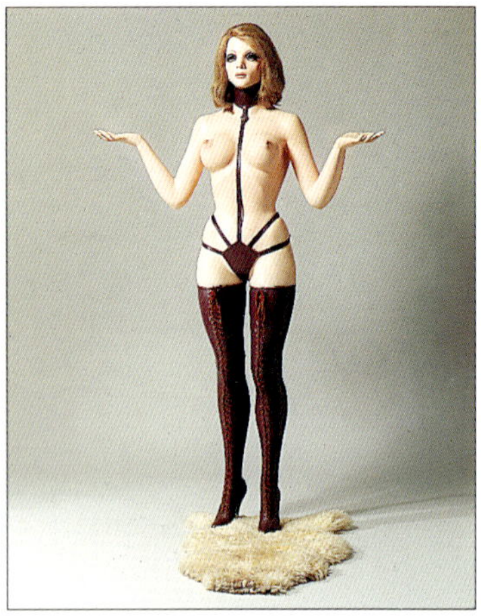

Allen Jones, Hat Stand, *1969, mixed media*

I think the art education system has been messed around with here in a way that's political. I haven't actually been involved with teaching here for years, though a teaching situation did enable me to live abroad for great lengths of time. I do like the idea of living some period of time outside one's regular environment. You suddenly discover, particularly in one's formative years, that what you thought were universal truths are just local opinion. For me, New York just *was* art. You weren't there for any other reason and the only people you knew were through art. There was a great openness.

– *How much do you think you were affected by the American experience and that kind of friendly competition with artists there? Your work changed a lot during that period and got larger in scale, much bolder and harder in treatment.*

I was very fortunate to be there when the artists I had seen in reproduction – Lichtenstein, Rosenquist, Indiana, Johns, Rauschenberg – were still on the street. The incredible lack of privacy that fame brings had not yet made them withdraw. There was an incredible warmth. I imagine that any young artist with the balls to go and look will most likely find the same situation in spite of big business and big money, which is now a yardstick for success but in the post-war period was something that you didn't particularly think about or expect.

Critical acclaim was pretty fantastic; that was also something which one hadn't particularly thought about and I think it might have just been an accident in a way for my generation – the group of artists you mentioned at the college. One had critical acclaim and started to represent one's country in exhibitions abroad straight out of art school. The notion of unremitting struggle before there was that sort of pay-off wasn't a part of our experience and the ability to meet and extend oneself through interaction with artists whom you admired was terrific. But for me, though I had got to know many of the artists mentioned very well, I found that, over the years, the artists I sought out would be either much older or artists whose work was on the other side of the planet from my own obsessions; that was the interesting thing, that it was possible to make those connections. For me, Ad Reinhardt and Newman were very important people.

– *It's been very tempting for a lot of critics of Pop art to read social and political messages into it in terms of consumerism and in terms of lifestyle in the 1960s and so forth. You've always tended to talk about your own work in very formal terms and almost never even to mention subject matter. It seems to me that the one area which has been most problematic for you in terms of your critics has been your treatment of sexuality, which actually does have quite a lot to do with changing attitudes in the 1960s. To what extent was it a conscious thing to introduce that as subject matter in your work? You knew that it would get certain reactions, you wanted reactions to it, positive and negative or whatever, but I'm sure you didn't expect quite the reactions that you got ten years later.*

Bill Copley, a great collector and an artist, said once that everybody's only required to like art, if you don't like it you can go away, you don't have to look at it. I suppose that through my American experience and through my own interest in wanting to paint the figure, I gradually learned a language which came from outside fine art sources, the adult comic strip and cartoons – things in which all the clutter of art didn't exist. If they didn't come through with the goods or make the point, then they wouldn't get the job next week. I'd been guest-teaching in Germany, Chicago and Los Angeles and I had this feeling that if everyone took their coffee break in the morning and you could swap everybody's drawings around between these three very different places, people would come back and just go on with the life-drawing. The teaching informed my own attitude towards the figure: I wanted to galvanise students into realising that life-drawing wasn't some sort of convention which was to do with trying to produce something that looked like all the other art that had been produced through the years. You had to create some interaction between yourself and the figure; one had to do something that was worthwhile for oneself. I realised that a lot of people, particularly young students, are embarrassed about the kind of stuff they like doing at home or by showing people their obsessions, or using imagery of the figure which had everything to do with the real world and their daily experience but nothing to do with the life class. It became a way through for me.

Through the 60s I gradually honed down a kind of emblematic way of portraying the female figure. And it became obvious even to me that I was making this figure more and more rendered and solid and that if I really wanted to test the water I should try and make this painted image into an object, to make it *real*. I had the first sculpture made by a fabricator. I had it made because it wasn't about the expressionist involvement of my thumb in the clay. This first sculpture was a standing figure, and I realised that it might just be possible that people would think it had something to do with Surrealism or a found object or a window mannequin or something, and so I needed to dislocate the presentation to make an impact which the viewer would have to confront personally and make up their own minds about. I'd seen in some comic somewhere the idea of people posing as furniture, and I used that. But the fact that ten years later, 20 years later, it was seen as some sort of political or socially wilful decision was not either a part of its inception or even a part of my interests. I think the artist's responsibility ends when he's got the work onto the wall, into the world. Things are going to be used and abused by people according to the experience they bring to the image. Certainly I created a strong image that was taken to represent the antithesis of my feelings towards women. But when I look around me in the street, or in this audience I see people who look just like my work, as if I had invented them. I just think that women look beautiful.

Allen Jones, Sheer Magic*, 1967, oil, 91x91cm*

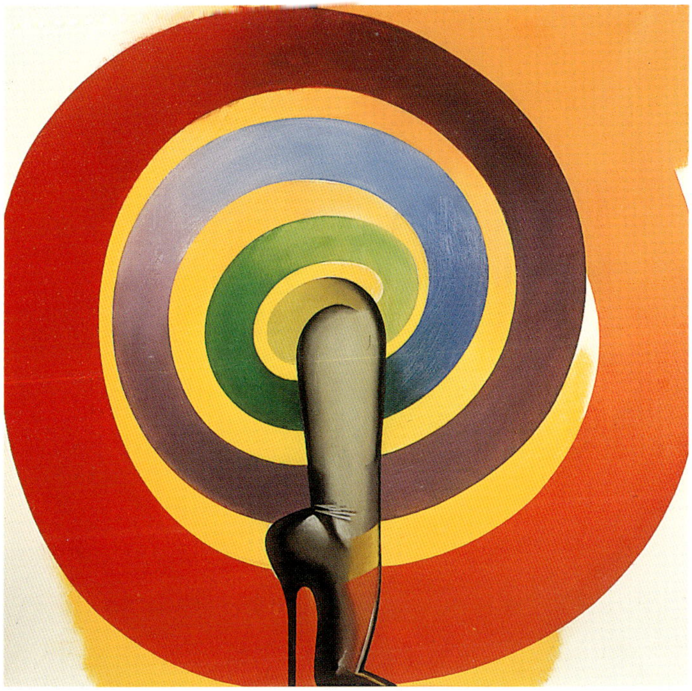

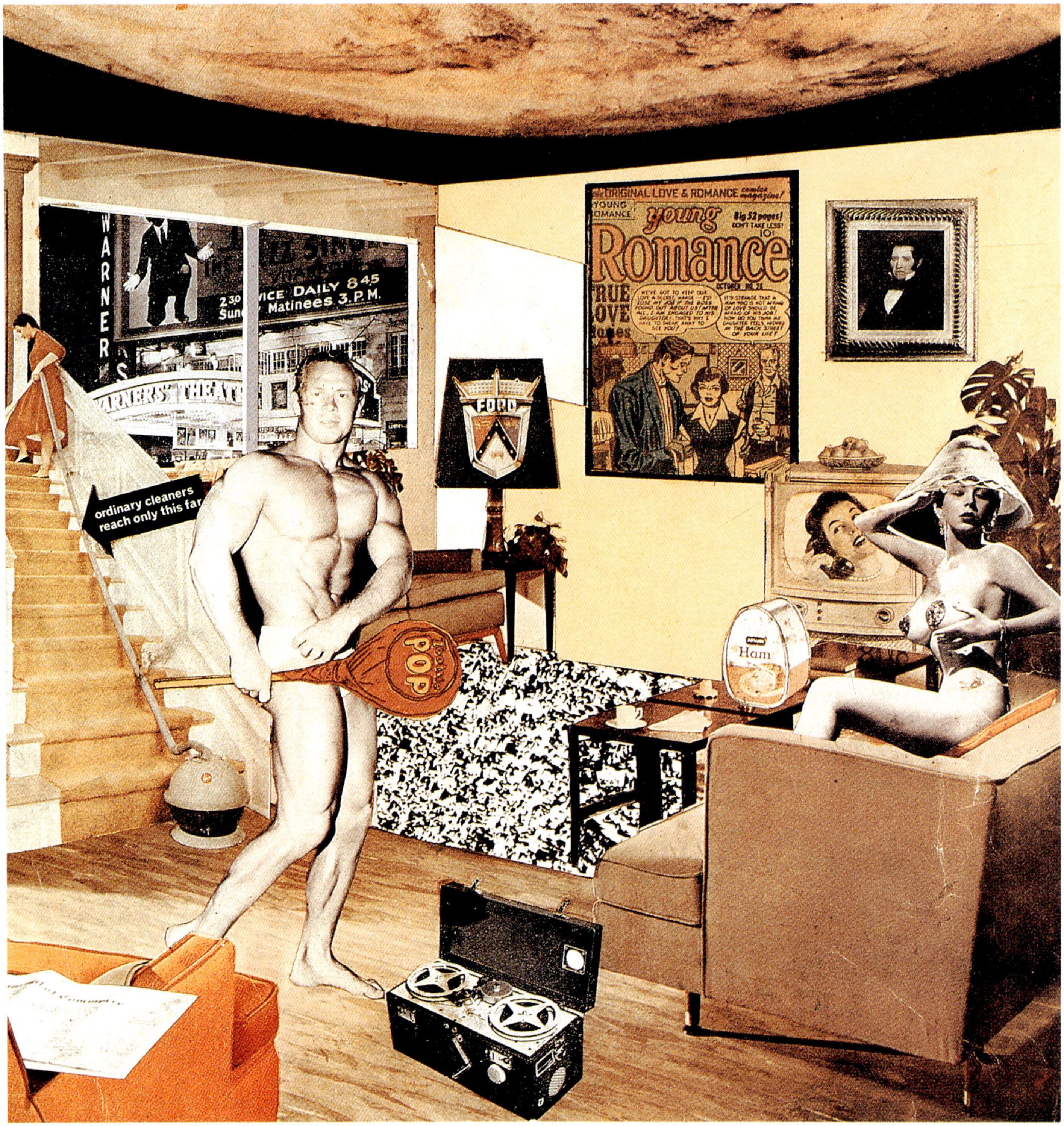
ORIGINAL LOVE & ROMANCE comics magazine!
YOUNG ROMANCE
young Romance
Big 52 pages! DON'T TAKE LESS!
10¢
ordinary cleaners reach only this far
WARNER
Sunday Matinees 3 P.M.
FORD
POP
Ham

RICHARD HAMILTON
INTERVIEWED BY RICHARD CORK

Richard Hamilton, Just what is it that makes today's homes so different, so appealing?, *1956, collage on paper, 26x25cm*

Richard Cork: *Richard, it was fascinating for me at the show yesterday, to be confronted in the first room by a whole body of American work which seemed to be opening up a whole range of hitherto unconsidered possibilities. Then to proceed to the second room and to find your work and that of Peter Blake and other artists in this country. It's a very provocative way to begin a show, because you immediately start to think not only about the common factors but also about the differences. I wanted to start by asking you whether, at the time of those early works in the 50s, you had any inkling of what was going on in the first room?*

Richard Hamilton: No, not a clue. We were completely isolated here from the work that was going on in New York, other than Abstract Expressionism, or I suppose in the mid 50s, hard-edged abstraction. You were either a hard-edged abstractionist or you were a dribbler and that was about it. Those were the options.

– *So where did you see yourself situated with regard to that kind of challenge?*

I didn't see myself situated at all, I felt completely out on a limb; I thought that I was being tremendously adventurous and alone, going out into the sea with absolutely nothing in front of me. There was a lot in the past, of course, and the basis for my thinking I suppose was that I had done two exhibitions that in some ways started off the idea that artists could make didactic shows about things that interested them. In 1951 I held an exhibition called 'Growth and Form', which was about the natural world, then in 1953 I had another exhibition, 'Man, Machine and Motion', which was about human beings and how they move in their environment; how they add things to themselves, vehicles of all sorts, a couple of simple bits of board on your feet and you're skiing on water. I tried to do things that were about space, about the way that people move in space. It was part of a genuine interest in perception at that time. I can't say that I was absorbed in Arnheim, but I did value greatly a book which came from America by a man called Gibson, *Perception of the Visual World.* It was a fascinatingly interesting small booklet about visual clues: how people on trapezes saw the ground and how they related to it. He said that it was very important to establish the rigging so that the two trapezes were absolutely level and were related to a level ground. If the ground wasn't level, then it could be disaster. Gibson examined all the facts and it turns out that when accidents occurred with trapeze artists, it was because the ground wasn't perfectly flat. So it's not just a question of moving about up there, it's a question of knowing your relationship to the ground.

So all sorts of perceptual clues became interesting to me and I just examined them in a very thorough, systematic and obviously scientific way; I tried to understand the experience of moving in a train and looking at a certain point. Then I felt that everything that I was doing, which was a kind of schematic way of describing motion, was related to normal perspective. It just became much more

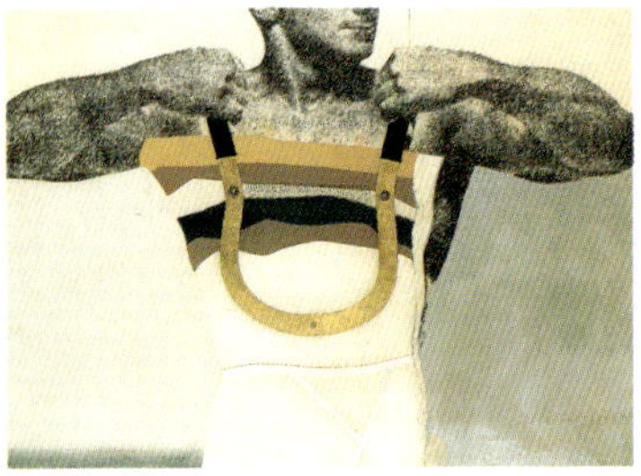

Richard Hamilton, Towards a definitive statement on the coming trends in men's wear: Adonis in Y fronts, *1962, oil and collage on panel, 61x81cm*

complicated. And then I tried to put objects in, say, a car moving in the opposite direction to a train. Around this time in the early 50s there was all this stuff going on at the Independent Group. But that was also very systematic and analytical and related in some ways to those two exhibitions. For example, the 'Man, Machine and Motion' exhibition was in close collaboration with Reyner Banham, who was thoroughly interested in American automobile styling, and he wrote very smart, snappy captions for the catalogue annotating each of the items. There was a great deal of encouragement in the Independent Group to study further, so we were given the book of the week to read, which might turn out to be very difficult. It might be on Cybernetics, on Information Theory or on Theory of Games and it got very tough. When Lawrence Alloway was involved we really scratched our heads over these books and we were then expected after two weeks of study to discuss them. It was like a sort of Open University on a small scale but there was very little discussion of art.

–Why did you think it was best to avoid discussing art?

The things that we discussed were cinema, pop records even, but there was a whole area of interest which almost required the avoidance of art; there was something in our makeup which made us do that. I was teaching from 1953 onwards and I tried to avoid talking to my students about art. It was always, if you do this something happens, it was trying to make the mind take over and it wasn't necessary to point to art. That would be saying that there is some stylistic mode that you should adopt, and I always see that as dangerous. I think the same sort of thing pervaded the Independent Group discussions: we weren't really interested in artistic styles, but in what was happening in the world, and I think it paid off.

– Certainly. Within the Independent Group, there was almost an obsession with things American, wasn't there?

Yes, that was because Britain was in a very deprived condition after the war. If you'd been in a factory, you probably would have spent some time making a lighter out of a bullet and a flint. The most desirable possession after the war was a real lighter, a Zippo was really macho. That I think was the attitude with just about everything. You hankered after a Whirlpool washing machine and you drooled over pages of advertising in *Good Housekeeping* and at *Esquire* for all the snappy clothes. The equivalent here was *Picture Post*, which is good, straight, documentary journalism, but it didn't have the glamour of *Life* magazine.

– Although you were drooling, what fascinates me about that surprisingly small collage Just what is it that makes today's homes so different, so appealing? *is the element of send-up in it. You are at one and the same time fascinated by and also satirising many of the preoccupations of what came to be known later on as Pop art.*

I don't think *sending up* is satirising and I don't think of it as drooling. I was drooling over the pages of the magazines, but I wasn't trying to get across this idea of drooling over it. I was trying to get somewhere right in the middle between these two possibilities of *glorifying* and *sending up*. Different people from different backgrounds have accused me of satirising America: the cultural attaché at the

American Embassy came to my house and was really curious to know why I was so unpleasant about America. English critics would say there was a mid-Atlantic tone of voice in my work. So it was hard to please everybody, but part of the ethos of the Independent Group, along with Information Theory and Theory of Games, was non-Aristotelian logic, which I took into my soul as a fascinating, new, philosophical possibility where you didn't say things were bad and you didn't say things were good – they were just there. I uphold this principle all the way through until I come to someone like Margaret Thatcher and you think, 'She's bad.' You must have some value judgements; I wouldn't go the whole hog and say everything has to be neutral. But at that time, I was interested in the aesthetic possibility of something which was completely neutral. And that's the explanation for that work; it was a kind of summary of the things that we'd all been thinking about, our group's contribution to 'This is Tomorrow'.

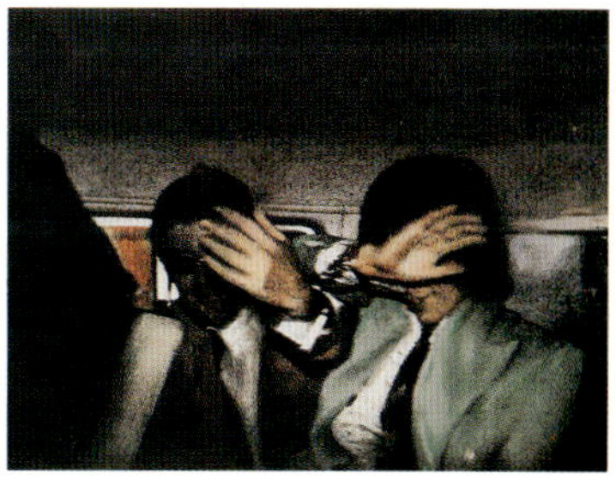

Richard Hamilton, Swingeing London 67 II, *1968, oil and silkscreen, 67x85cm*

– *That's the exhibition at the Whitechapel Art Gallery in 1956.*

Yes, which one always sees as the summation and termination of the Independent Group. Our contribution was not only about pop culture – Wurlitzer disk players, that sort of thing – but it was also about perception. This even went back to my 1951 interest in the way we see things. I persist in being interested in the two strands: you express things in a visual language which people understand or not. And in that visual language, what are the images and icons which you're using, what myths are being expressed?

– *Of course it's strange the way in which the grinding processes of art history get going.* Just what is it *is often seen as some kind of presentiment, even a begetter of Pop art. Whereas in fact it was very much tied in with that particular exhibition; you wouldn't have seen it in 1956 as any kind of christening of a new movement would you?*

Oh no, not at all. In fact I didn't show it in a gallery context until 64, at the Hanover Gallery. I tried for eight years to persuade dealers around London to give me an opportunity to show. I would have shown that picture at any time between 56 and my next show in 64.

– *You mean they simply weren't interested?*

No, I couldn't persuade the gallery who had given me my first show to come up to Highgate and take a look at what I was doing. Putting it on the shelf for those years didn't mean that I wasn't interested in it, and when I put it in the show, it made sense of the work that I'd done between 1957-62.

To go back to your original question, I felt myself to be in total isolation up until something like 61, when Lawrence Alloway said there are some interesting kids at the college, and I learned about the existence of Peter Blake, Allen Jones and David Hockney in particular. And then somebody arranged an exhibition in a little gallery on Cork Street or somewhere, which consisted mainly of people from the Royal College. And I don't know how anyone knew of my existence even, but I was very pleased that I was invited to contribute.

– *Did you feel that you belonged in that context?*

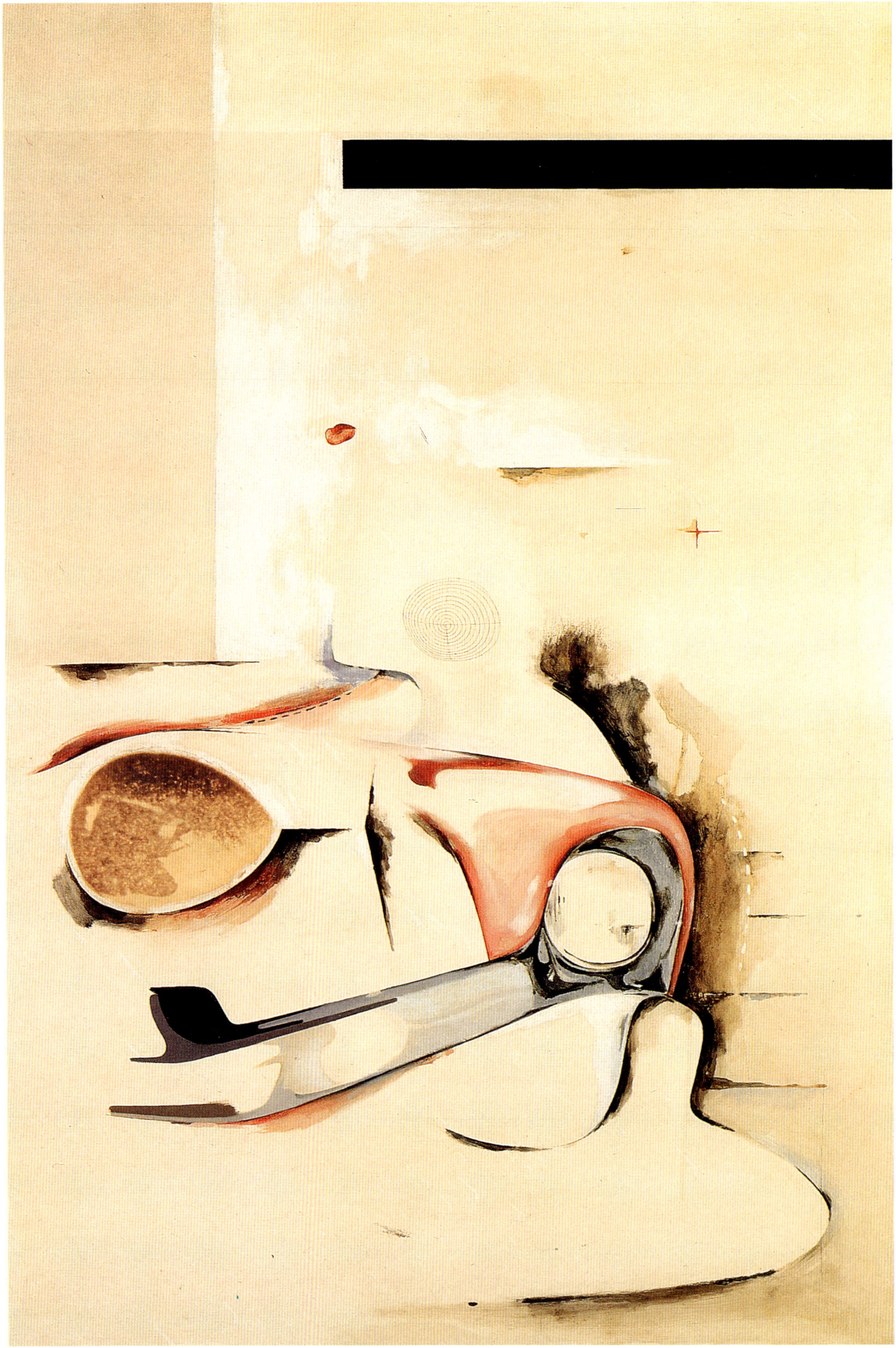

No, I felt as though I was of the older generation in a way. I was anything up to ten years older than most of them. I was rather pleased, as I think of it. I was carried along on David Hockney's golden coat-tails. He wafted in and I was somehow given a little reflected shine from this gold suit that he wore on special occasions.

Richard Hamilton, Hommage à Chrysler Corp, *1957, oil, metal, foil and collage on panel, 122x81cm*

– *Of course, he's always said that he was nothing to do with Pop art; in fact he made a public statement to that effect at one point in the 60s, didn't he?*

Well, I've never chosen to deny it. But there have been disclaimers. Paolozzi made a famous disclaimer, 'I am not responsible for Pop art.' I think it was at the last meeting of the Independent Group, which I didn't attend for some reason; I don't think I was invited.

– *You talked about the British manifestation of Pop; what about its American manifestation? When did you first become aware of what was going on in New York?*

The first sign of it was an exhibition at the ICA of American painting in the early 60s. I think those were probably the first Pollocks to be shown in London and the first Warhols; and Warhol was a knock-out. The end wall of the Dover Street ICA was covered with 30 or 40 of the great early Marilyns.

– *This would have been about 1962? And it certainly wasn't done under the banner of Pop in any way at all?*

No, it was just New York and it was paid for by Peter Watson, one of the original sponsors of the ICA. He was a wonderful rich young man who paid for Horizon all the way through the war and helped the ICA afterwards. He was motivated to get this exhibition over and it was an absolute flop. He was very depressed about it because it had been quite a big venture for him to do, and a lot of effort and a great deal of money had been expended and it sank like a stone as far as critical work was concerned. But it was a very powerful experience to see.

– *We heard earlier from Allen Jones about how difficult it was in a way for an art student to actually find out about Pollock or whoever. When did you first go to America to find what we think of as American Pop art?*

I knew Jasper Johns slightly from a lecture that we did at the ICA – one of the few lectures there concerned with art – which was a triple talk with three members of the Independent Group: Anthony Hill, Sandy Wilson and myself. We had an interest in Duchamp. We didn't know much about it, but we thought it was worthwhile boning up and each doing a presentation. And I decided I would find out what was in the *Green Box*, since I couldn't speak French and couldn't read it. I'm the only monolingual translator in the business, I think. I'm always thought of as being the translator of the *Green Box*, but really I had to get somebody to give me the meaning of every word in the thing and then put it together. But this was quite an important moment for me; I began to work on a typographic version of the *Green Box*, which was eventually published in 1960.

– And how did Duchamp respond?

Well, I wrote to him after the lecture because I'd made a diagram of the 'Large Glass', and there were people in the audience who purported to know about Duchamp, one of whom said we were absolutely stupid and Duchamp would have thought we were crazy. So I sent my diagram which I'd been working on for weeks and weeks to Duchamp with a little note saying, 'Could you tell me what's wrong with it?' I didn't hear a word from him until almost exactly a year later when I got a letter in this familiar handwriting that I'd been pouring over in the *Green Box*. And it said that a professor of art history at Yale called George Heard Hamilton (no relation) had done a little collection of jottings on the *Green Box* and would I collaborate with him on a complete English version. He didn't mention my chart and never did subsequently. My publication was reviewed. There were very few reviews of this book but one of them, strangely, was written by Jasper Johns in a one-issue New York underground newspaper called *Scrap*. He wrote a beautiful little review, not of the book so much as of his approach to Duchamp. He ended this piece by saying he was reminded of a cartoon in *The New Yorker* where two cavemen are sitting there and one says to the other, 'OK, so he invented fire. Then what did he do?' Most artists of my generation who I feel close to share that attitude towards Duchamp. He invented fire.

– Duchamp has been popping up – excuse the pun – all morning hasn't he? Can you just try and summarise why Duchamp was important to you? It's not really been explained how he contributed to Pop art.

I don't know that it was a contribution to Pop art, but this interest is really persistent. I made friendships all over America and in Paris, largely through Bill Copley, who had lots of contacts. But it was always through an enthusiasm for Duchamp. I met people like Jean Tinguely with Duchamp; I went to America for the first time because I'd been working with Duchamp, corresponding practically weekly for years. When I went from New York to Pasadena I sat beside Marcel on the plane and we travelled all the way across America and he pointed out Massachusetts to me three times. He was very interested in maps, Marcel. And then when we got to Pasadena, there were all these people there, Andy Warhol was having a show at Irving Blum's gallery, there was a magnificent show of Oldenburg at the Dwan Gallery, Billy Al Bengston was there and five or six other people were all having shows there. But the arrival of Duchamp was treated like a feast, it was incredible, like a young occasion. The kids really made it a riot, the enthusiasm for Duchamp was extraordinary.

– And how did Duchamp respond to this?

He loved it. He liked to be fêted, strangely enough. He was thought of as being very retiring, but I think he enjoyed the admiration that all these young people had for him.

– What about your own attitude towards Warhol and Lichtenstein and the others? How did you react to that when you first saw them?

I thought they were wonderful because they, especially Warhol, seemed to be doing something that I thought was quite impossible. When I made my suggested list of characteristics of Pop art, all these things like glamour, youth, wit, big business, all these characteristics which could be identified in Elvis Presley seemed to me to be not incompatible with fine art – you can see it, Rubens was pretty glamorous. But I thought that records were made for very temporary consumption; they were transitory and expendable. I thought, that's not fine art. Popular art is expendable, but fine art relies for its being on the idea of permanence, and it's preserved by other people who believe in that idea. And then when I went to America I thought, he's done it, good for him. He's proved me wrong. Warhol made an art designed for a short life. Who would have thought that people would collect Brillo boxes and that they would end up at museums, the Royal Academy? So it wasn't really Andy who made this big leap, he made the big leap in doing it, but the people who made the biggest leap were the museum officials who realised that this was a great man, a great artist and the stuff was good.

– *Were you shocked in any way by the work?*

No, I thought it was marvellous. The show in Irving Blum's was the silver Elvis Presley. It isn't a big gallery, but the first room was just completely covered with Elvis Presley. He just got this big canvas, painted it with silver paint, got a silk screen and started pulling his squeegee all the way along with black, overlapping them sometimes to leave little gaps, but I think it was done in a very arbitrary kind of way. For the show at Irving Blum's, he had one of these lengths, like a silk-screen-printed textile you buy by the metre and he just cut them up and they were put on stretchers, sometimes double Elvis and sometimes single Elvis. I'd seen the Marilyn Monroe painting, but the first sign of a freshly-made Warhol was in that exhibition. I was just tagging along with Marcel everywhere. He was treated like royalty, and I was treated not like a Prince exactly, but someone associated with the court.

The back room where the public didn't normally go was full of Liz Taylor paintings, and then in Irving Blum's office there were the Campbell's soup cans, which were little paintings, one of every flavour. Irving Blum had sold one and had bought it back because he realised that he had broken the set, and when we met him he was preening himself with the luck he'd had in getting it back. I think Warhol made a tremendous impact on me at that time, but it was because I thought that it was so extraordinary that he should have succeeded in this throw-away attitude. These things looked so casual, and yet they were obviously magnetic presences.

– *He made an impact on you, but did he change your art, or, in your knowledge, that of any other British artists?*

He changed it only in the sense that the first things I did when I got back home were a thing I called *My Marilyn*, because there had been lots of Marilyns before, and the *Epiphany* disc, which was a direct response to California, though not directly to Warhol's work. Irving Blum took me to Billy Al Bengston's studio in Venice, California. There's a big place there which is the West Coast equivalent of Coney Island, and I thought how marvellous it was that it should be called Pacific Ocean Park: POP. We went to this little joke shop and there were statues of hands and every kind of vulgar monstrosity and among them a disc which said 'Slip it to Me', which was the only thing I purchased in there. I just magnified it, but it was really to show my understanding. It could be thought of as a kind of Pop-Duchampian thing, to make an enlargement of a ready-made, but it also has more to do with the feeling that the kind of imagery made by the American artists ought to be recognised and established in a work.

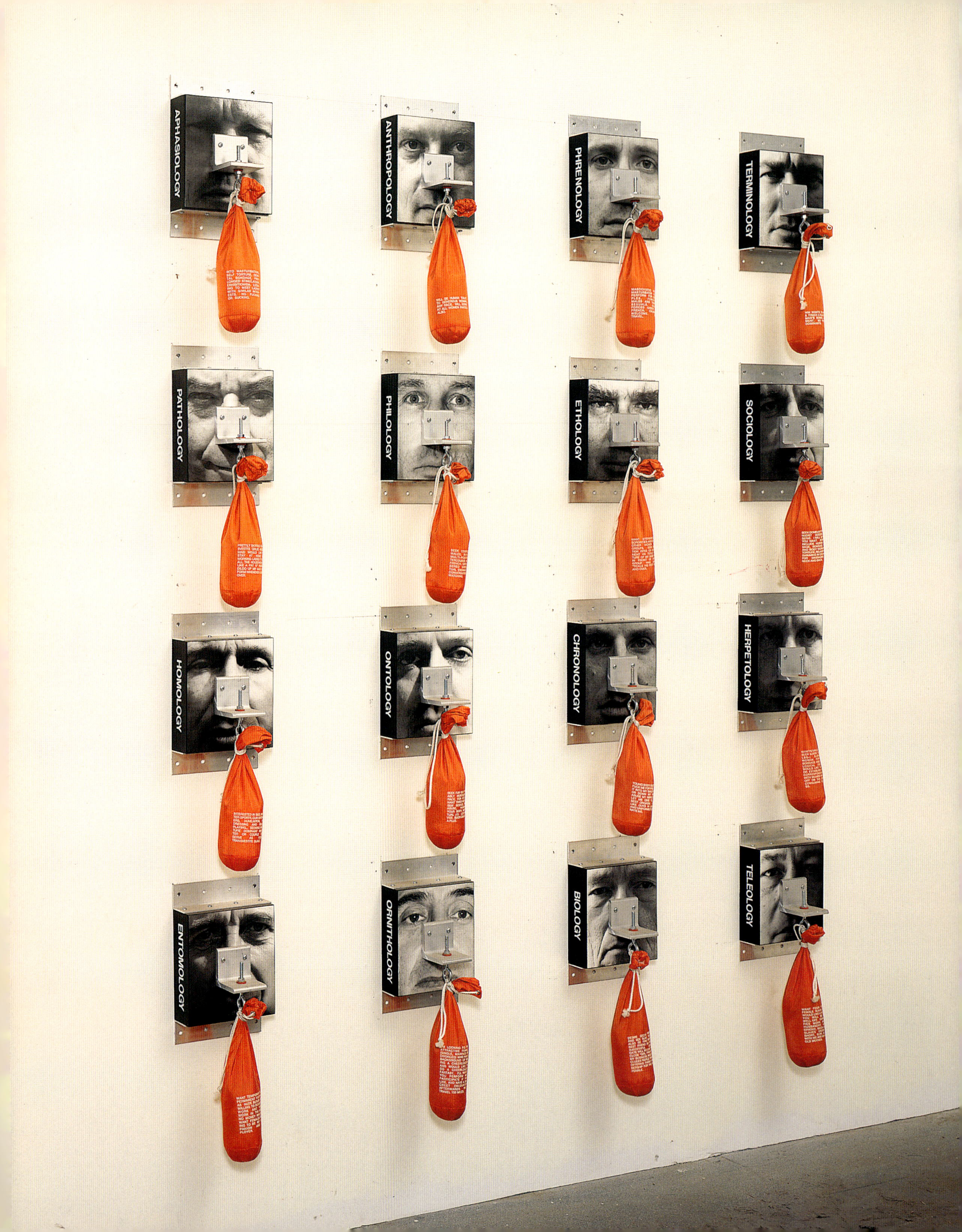
APHASIOLOGY
ANTHROPOLOGY
PHRENOLOGY
TERMINOLOGY
PATHOLOGY
PHILOLOGY
ETHOLOGY
SOCIOLOGY
HOMOLOGY
ONTOLOGY
CHRONOLOGY
HERPETOLOGY
ENTOMOLOGY
ORNITHOLOGY
BIOLOGY
TELEOLOGY

DAN CAMERON
A BRIDGE BETWEEN TWO SHOWS: POP AND REAL POP

I was brought up in the 60s, and when I learnt about art for the first time it was through the paintings of Roy Lichtenstein. I had some vague sense that other kinds of art had been done prior to the 60s, but I was not interested in that, because once I saw Pop art as a product of American culture, Pop art really was art. For a child of the 60s, there was no other way of conceiving of art at that time because culture seemed to be one large entity rather than separate categories. If the exhibition at the Royal Academy shows anything, it shows the beginnings of a time when art with a small *a* and art with a large *A* actually began to separate from one another. And it's been my feeling for a long time that it did not kill painting, which is an early 20th-century metaphor concerning patricide, the way the avant-garde gains ground by killing off its fathers. I think that was a very workable myth for a long time in the 20th century but it is not any more, and the reason for that is Pop art.

Today, it seems to me that all art is also Pop art. I look at different types of painting, photography and mass-media work and it seems that artists today, especially of my generation or younger, grew up in a similar environment, where Andy Warhol, for example, was a cultural figure whose importance went way beyond the boundaries of galleries and museums. His art was a statement about the all-inclusiveness of culture, the way that parts that had been separated could be linked up together.

When I came to New York in 1979, the first serious thing that I noticed was a young painter named Jed Garret, who was scandalously young and who created very fey, sloppy paintings, in hot contrasting colours of Greek statuary; 'limp Greek statuary' with lots of curlicues and scalloping around the edges. His was a very antagonistic position to be taking at the end of the 70s when art was concerned with process, abstraction and conceptualism. As the art world broke into the 80s, there was a fervent move towards painting. That was something that troubled me at the time because I couldn't – and still can't – see the qualities in some of those 'painterly' American painters. But there was another movement going on at the same time, which has become the most characteristic American movement of the last 15 years, and that is the photo-conceptual school, or what is sometimes referred to as the Metro Pictures School, since all of the artists who were of that ilk either show at or showed at the gallery Metro Pictures in New York.

What those artists of the early 80s were doing was taking the strategies of John Baldessari, William Wegman and other photo-conceptual but more documentation-oriented artists of the 70s. They continued to expand photography, pushing it away from the idea that the photograph documents the world; the photograph instead becoming a replica or a remnant of culture's own self-reflexiveness. So what the quintessential artists in that movement were doing – Barbara Kruger, Sherrie Levine, Richard Prince, Allan McCollum to some extent, Louise Lawler, Cindy Sherman – was recasting popular culture as a critical entity. They were making copies of photographs, of photographs from advertisements, blowing up graphic imagery and very carefully laying out type in such a way as to give their images a great deal of punch. There hadn't been such a concern for the purely visual in American art for some time. But it took several years for this group to get its legs because the painting movement was so

Ashley Bickerton, (As yet Untitled), *1991, aluminium, wood, photo etching, nylon and sand, 228.6x172.72x15.24cm*

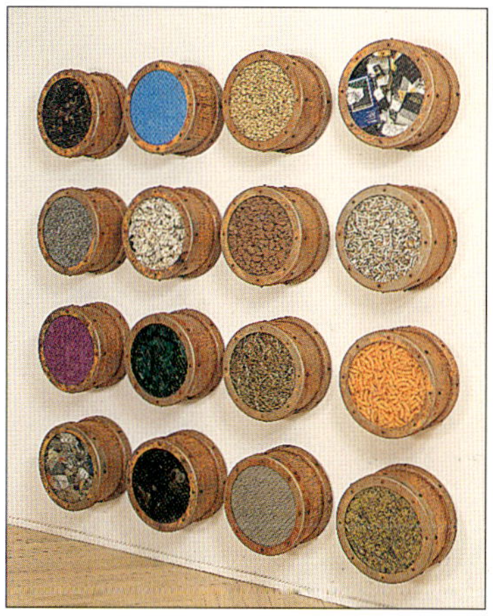

Ashley Bickerton, Catalog: Terra Firma Nineteen Hundred Eighty Nine #3, *1990, peppers, copper sulphate, pebbles, polaroid film trash, metal shavings, coral, red rocks, cigarettes, purple pigment, glass, straw, cheese doodles, trash, hair, sand, lichen, 223.5x223.5x25.4cm*

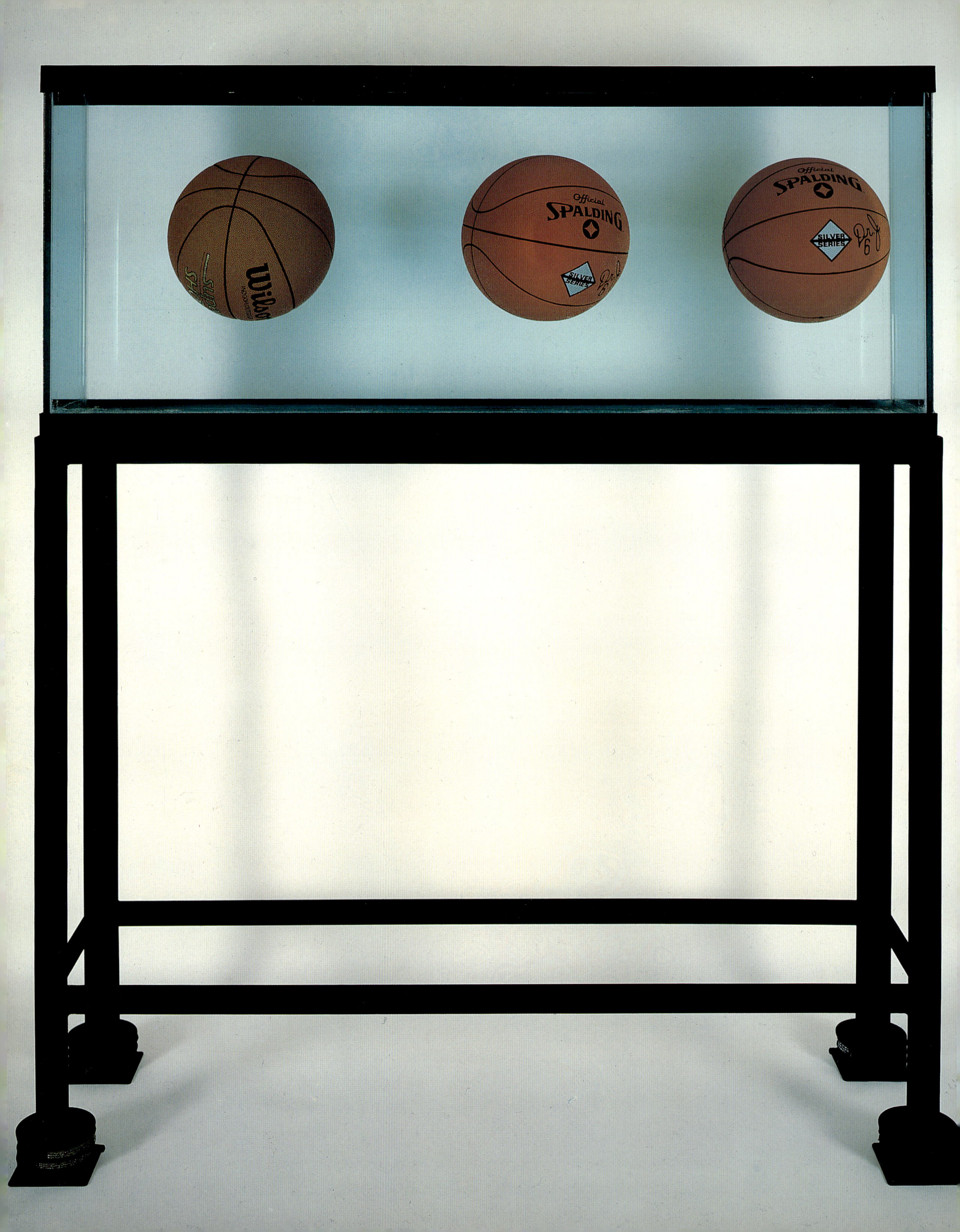
Wilson
Official
SPALDING
SILVER SERIES
Official
SPALDING
SILVER SERIES

dominant in New York at the time.

Now one thing that intrigues me, which I am sure many people have noticed in the Pop Art exhibition or the Serpentine Gallery, and what seems to have changed is that the early 60s were incredibly sexist times. The art was a product of that environment just as we are of our times and there was a certain use of the image of the woman in art and also a certain exclusion of the woman as artist throughout that whole period, and it seems to me that that was the last stand for this kind of exclusively male-dominated thinking in art. I don't know why that was so, and it occurs to me that you could never have that situation today where of 87 artists, only one is a woman. Over the last ten years, especially in New York, most of the very interesting, pioneering artists of this conceptual restatement of photography were women. I think there was a reason why women artists at that time went to the periphery, to photography, the technique of appropriation, the use of commercial graphics in order to make a statement that was somehow subversive.

In 1981 I walked into the Mary Boone Gallery, then a very up-and-coming small gallery, and there was a piece on the wall: a fluorescent light element with a vacuum cleaner stuck to it. I hadn't been shocked in quite that way by anything since I'd arrived in New York, and I was told that this was a sculpture by Jeff Koons, who was very young and very smart, and who was having his first show there in the spring. A little later I heard of a fantastic sculpture at Annina Nosei's by a young artist named Jeff Koons, who was having his first exhibition there in the spring . . . Neither of these exhibitions actually happened, which immediately endeared me to that artist: he had pitted two rivals against each other and ruined his chances for a show for what turned out to be about five years. Koons is not the sort of artist one would think of as making an anti-commercial statement, but that's not what that was about.

Koons' 1985 exhibition of sports-related sculpture – the tanks with the floating basket ball and the bronzed sports equipment – marked for me the day everything changed in New York. There was a great flurry of excitement, with people calling each other saying, 'You've got to get over there, this artist is floating basketballs in a tank, it's the strangest thing you'll ever want to see.'

Up until then Julian Schnabel had dominated everything with his bombast and his incredible ego and his incredible superficiality. Suddenly he was meaningless, he didn't have a role anymore. Koons was the one who put his finger on the need to find a new of way of coming up with meaning in contemporary art, and I think that he's been doing that consistently ever since.

In about the same year, Ashley Bickerton had his first show, at the Cable Gallery. I remember thinking it was very clever and very finished, and I wrote a review for *Flash Art*. I didn't know Ashley Bickerton, but somebody introduced us and he said, 'I read what you wrote about me,' and I thought, 'Well I didn't say anything too bad, maybe he's pleased.' I said, 'What did you think of the article?' and he said, 'Well it was interesting, but you didn't go into all the linguistic and anthropological aspects of my work!' It was not until a year or so later that I realised that even though the early works had seemed very superficial and very trivial, he was discovering very meaty material which I didn't see to begin with, and from that point on I was fascinated with both Ashley's work and his mind.

The point I have been trying to make early on is that I think Pop is a continuity. There will never be a moment when Pop is no longer part of the cultural horizon because I think it is the first manifestation of a new kind of art that will take us into the 21st century, and it is no less Pop-inflected than it was 30 years ago. As the worlds of high art and low culture converge, become the same thing, we no longer feel the need to declare something as art or not art. I think that art contains a lot of different possibilities, but its future lies in becoming merged with other forms of cultural expression.

Jeff Koons, Three Ball Total Equilibrium Tank, *1985, glass, iron, water, sodium chloride reagent, 3 basketballs, 154x124x34cm*

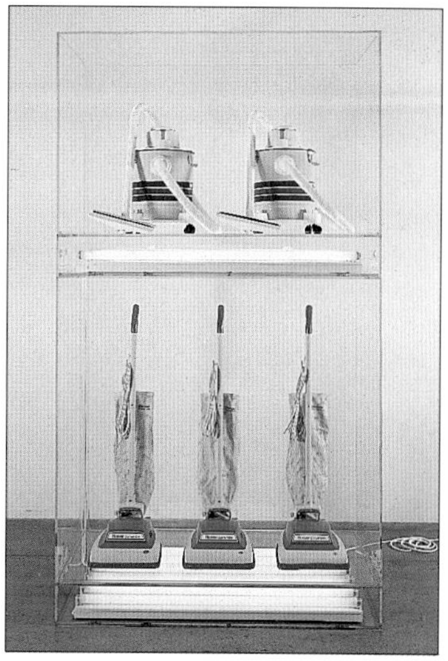

Jeff Koons, New Hoover Convertibles, New Shelton Wet/Drys Five-Gallon Doubledecker, *1981-87, three convertibles, five-gallon wet/drys, plexi, fluorescent tubes, 251.46x137.16x71.12cm*

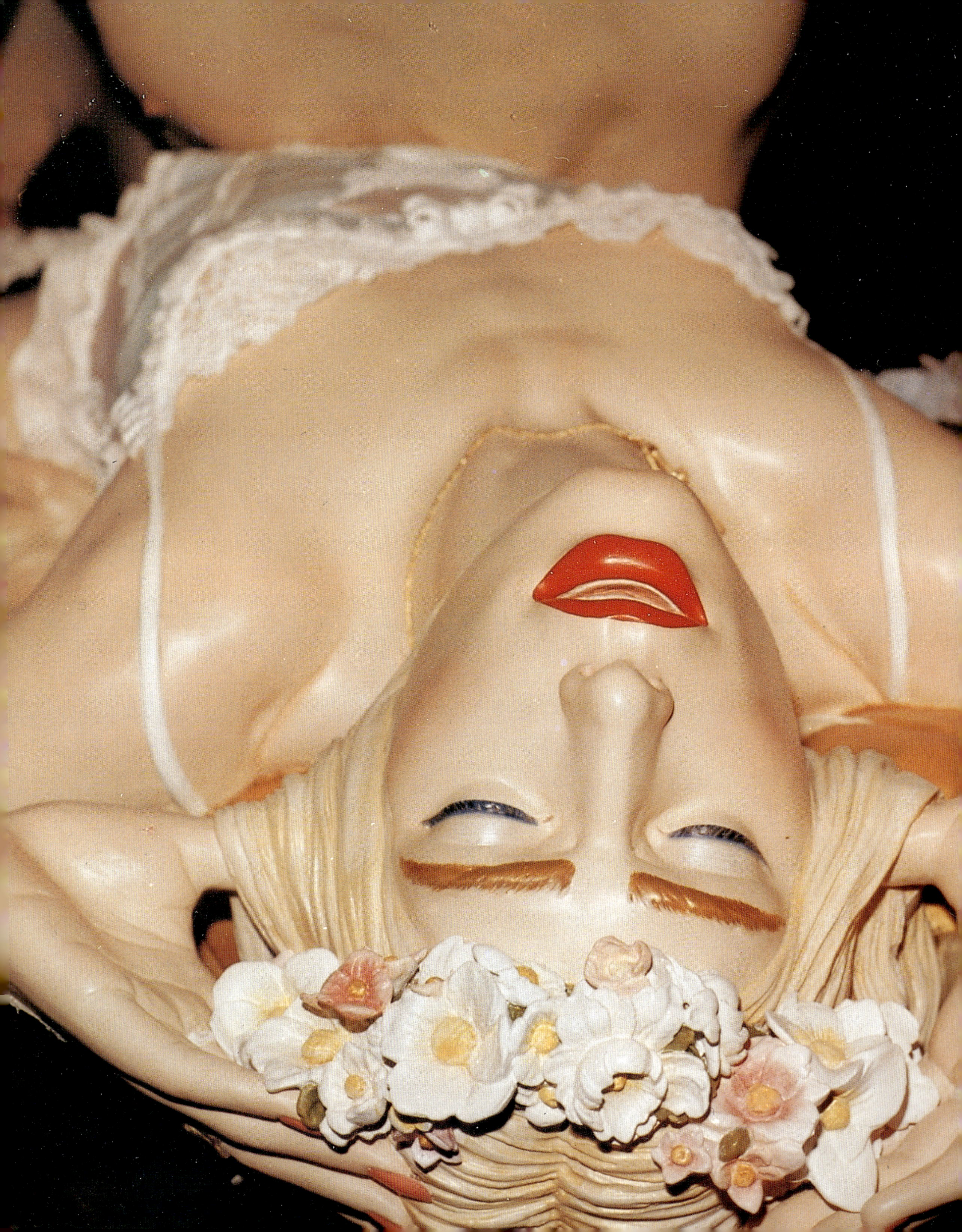

JEFF KOONS
INTERVIEWED BY MATTHEW COLLINGS

Jeff and Iona (Made in Heaven), *Venice Biennale, installation detail, 1990 (photo Andreas Papadakis)*

OVERLEAF: Ilona on Top (Rosa Background), *1990 (photo Riccardo Schicci), 'The whole body of work will redefine the definition of the perverse.'*

Matthew Collings: *Looking around the show here at the Royal Academy, what's so enjoyable is the sense of objects that have to make their own logic. Your* Winter Bears *at the Serpentine is very beautifully made, it's funny, you want to touch it, it's very precisely done – although of course you didn't make it. I wonder how your relationship to your work in terms of objects is different to the classic Pop art of the 60s.*

Jeff Koons: I think it's important to keep in mind that my father was an interior decorator. As I grew up, one room for one month would be a living room and another room would be a den or a bar-room, and then a month later it would be a kitchen. And I learned that objects and things in your environment affect you emotionally and change your perception of the world. Pop art to me has always seemed to want to use an objective vocabulary to communicate with people. Pop art is a movement that continues to transform itself and is the lifeblood of future contemporary art, I believe. It's a return to the objective where art met the needs of people.

My favourite Pop artist is Michelangelo, who by all definitions is a Pop artist because he dealt in a vocabulary which communicated to people. You look at his torso and this exaggeration of a muscle and think yes, I have a muscle here and you feel your body and start to listen to the world. You start to listen sexually, spiritually, and this is Pop art.

– *So you say the continuing factor is communication of the most vivid and the most immediate, the most immediately understandable statement.*

When people look at this popular vocabulary, they think it's simplistic. But to me something that is articulated is just the opposite of simplistic.

– *Am I speaking for you now if I say that a statement which is able to sum up quite a complicated meaning in a very simple way is what's interesting to you?*

To use art, to exercise the power of the artist, to be in that state of perversion, to have the desire to lead when you know your limitation . . . that's the role that I see of the artist and the populist artist.

– *The agenda for these two shows seems to be to broaden the idea of what Pop art is. I would imagine the most set idea that most people have about Pop art is that it came in the 60s and was something to do with the everyday continuum as opposed to the rarefied art-world continuum. I'm still interested in the difference between Pop art say, in terms of Warhol, and what you do. What's the difference, perhaps let's put it this way, in making yourself a media personality when someone like Warhol has already done it?*

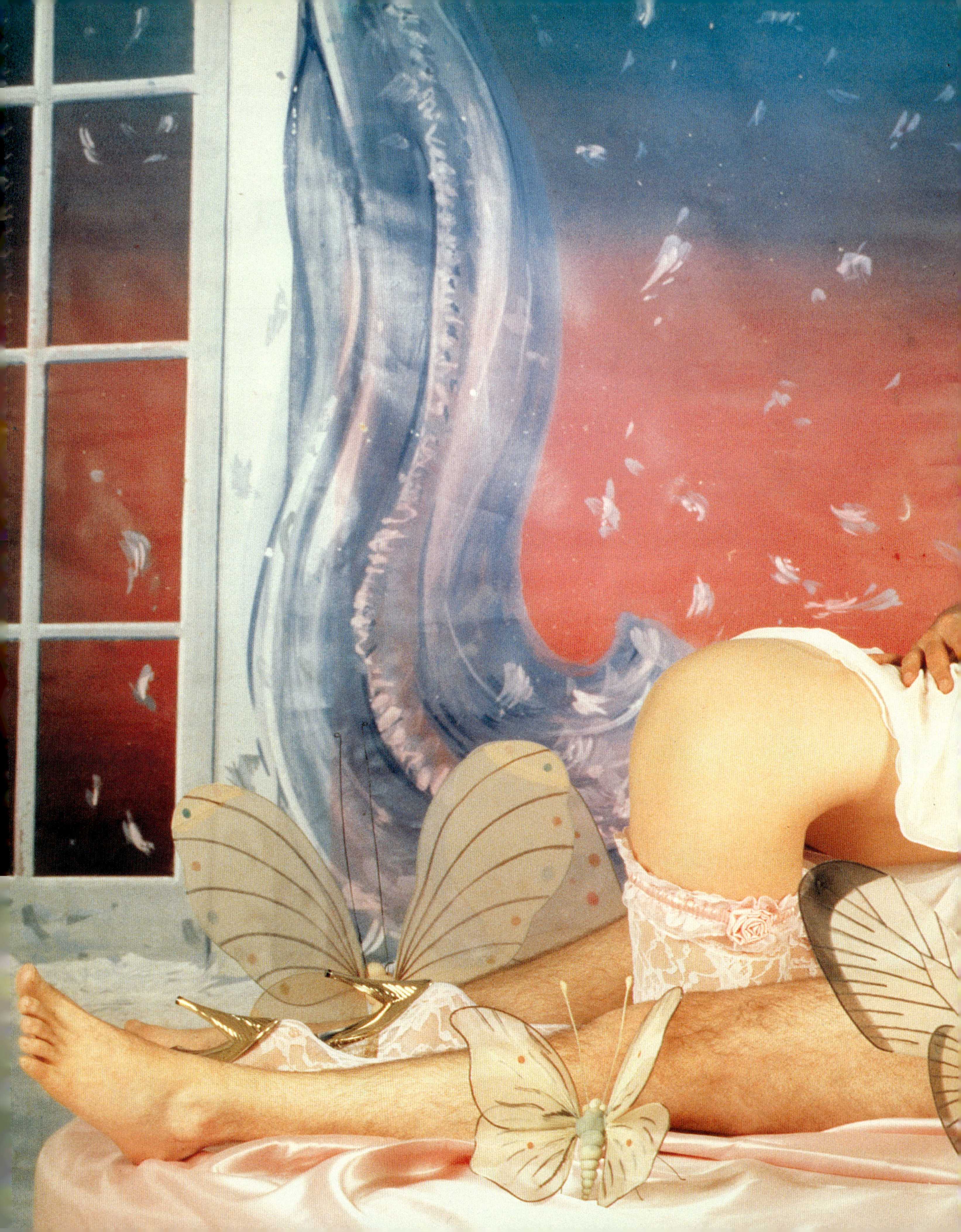

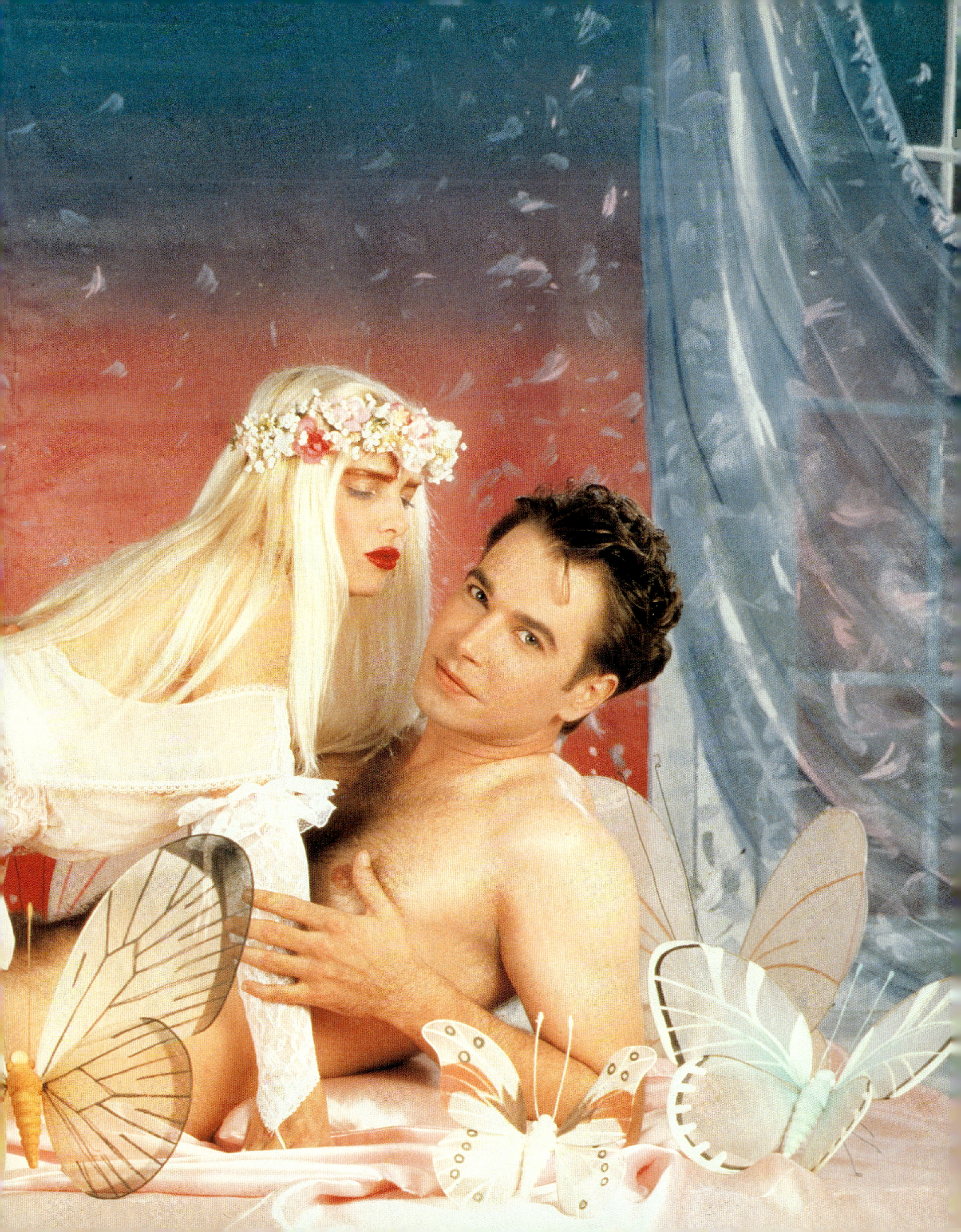

Marcel Duchamp is a great hero of mine and I think that most people involved in Pop art have filtered through him. Andy and I are very different in our sexuality, our desire and our need for love. I'm trying to make work that removes the important and the sophisticated from the world because Jeff Koons doesn't believe in the important or the sophisticated. I think Andy believed in both of these. I'm trying to make work that is levelling and lets people know that it's enough to be clever in the world, and if they embrace their past, they have a foundation to achieve their desires. I'm a self-made man and my wife Ilona is a self-made woman and we're both examples of this philosophy.

– *After Andy Warhol died, there was a certain amount of interest in whether there was a point where private Andy ended and public Andy began. Perhaps they were completely merged into one. In your own case, is there a conflict between the private Jeff who remembers home and father, and the public Jeff that we now know and are amazed by?*

I really don't have a lot of respect for the position of the artist, including myself. I deal with this contradiction every day. I try to expose myself as much as possible and to be as generous as possible. I love the perversion of going to one's limitation and still desiring to lead. My *Rabbit*, by the way, I have always seen as a symbol of that.

– *As a symbol of being a leader?*

Of being a leader, an orator, the carrot to the mouth is a symbol of masturbation. I see Pop art as feeding people a dialogue that they can participate in. Instead of the artist being lost in this masturbative act of the subjective, the artist lets the public get lost in the act of masturbation.

– *So, I think the answer to my question might be that it is possible to distinguish a private person here but that privateness is magically made public and connects with the privateness of everybody.*

I believe in simple things and I am a simple person. I reveal my simplicity and I act on my simplicity.

– *I first heard about you in early 1986 or so when you were one of a group of artists that included Ashley Bickerton and some other people. The ideas of appropriation and Baudrillard were going round. A couple of years later the new Jeff emerged with the Banality sculptures at Sonnabend, and there was a very funny article by Peter Schjeldahl which was really a kind of statement of admiration. He used phrases like, 'a combination of blazing social comment and perfect aesthetic pitch', and then he said, 'but at the same time this is work that makes you sick,' and this is ' twerpish art'. These were things that hadn't really been discerned in the more theoretical group of artists. I wonder if that was a conscious effort on your part to create a new person?*

I've tried consciously for quite some time. Before the Banality work there was the Equilibrium work. I try to make a body of work that performs similarly to television; it tells a story, there's a beginning, a middle and an end, and it opens itself up to absolutely everyone whatever their intellectual level would be. It's all about creating an equilibrium and a levelling effect where a flow of power can exist. I think one of the vehicles that I try to exploit most is that of social mobility. I tried to bring an upper class down and raise a lower class up. The equilibrium point is really the bourgeois: I believe totally in bourgeois standards, I believe that I have achieved that class. My wife and I are both very happy in this classical bourgeois state and we hope to give the direction and leadership to exploit opportunities in this entropy.

– *That was one of the best replies of the day. But the question, between that group of Banality sculptures and the previous works of the drink containers and the rabbit, was there a conscious decision to make a more expanded public figure out of Jeff Koons? You did become much more famous, you became more this outrageous person.*

I think what I invented more than my egoism was my courageousness. When I did the Banality work I stopped working with the object as a ready-made and assumed the public as a ready-made; I just pushed every button, I removed their options. If I wasn't going to seduce the public through sexuality I would seduce them with spirituality and if that didn't work, I would use materialism, and even an essence of formalism.

– *I think I heard this right, it's not the object that's the ready-made, even though someone else made it, but it's the public that's the ready-made . . . ?*

I use the artist as the ready-made in the execution of the object: I would find artists that I could exploit for what they do best. I always thought of *Winter Bears* as being a very Paul McCartney-style piece. If somebody wants to read that as a pop love song, they can, if it's a symbol of a sacred-hearted Jesus, they can read it as that. It will be a complete chameleon for you.

– *It's very precisely made, although you didn't make it yourself, you had to tell your artisans where the colour is.*

It's totally controlled. It's not that I send a drawing to somebody, they send it back and I sell it. I oversee everything and I'm sure that it has to do with an aspect of sexual control over my production people that I enjoy. The work, once you're involved in it, takes on certain personal meanings, but the first line of defence is that it's a total chameleon. These works also wanted to deal with the familiar; they didn't present themselves in a form which made the public feel guarded, it wanted to create a general sense of familiarity, where the imagery comes from airport shopping centres, postcards and popular magazines.

– *Of course, that sort of area is the one that sounds the most like Pop art. But this area about control, and some of the other things you said about your personality meeting the personality of the public, are not so familiar from the usual Pop art talk. Perhaps that's where what you do is more than just an exaggerated or up-dated version of Pop.*

I think it would be great if instead of reading that I am the new inheritor of Warhol, somebody would write 'the new Bernini'. I see Baroque as the last point in art history where artists dealt in the objective. Right now I'm also involved in six or eight copyright law suits dealing with the imagery that I work with.

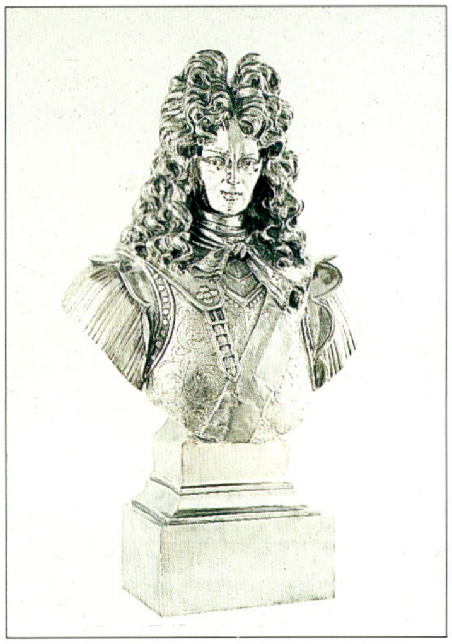

Louis XIV, *1986, cast stainless steel, 117x69x38cm. 'I think what I first enjoyed so much about the Baroque – I enjoyed the idea that the church used this and exploited it more than anyone – was that one's needs were met when they came into contact with this art. If you were hungry, you forgot that you had no money in your pocket and your stomach felt full for the moment and whatever position you were in you felt automatically a sense of social mobility and contact through it even though you were a peasant and would always be a peasant, there was always a sense of mobility through the Baroque and this is what has always attracted me. It deals with the rational and the irrational side by side, there is an equilibrium between the animate and the inanimate. I enjoy this state.'*

This is a visual vocabulary that has been taken away from me and of course it's been taken away from the public too. I don't believe in the restriction of that vocabulary. The laws concerning art right now are totally based on Modernism, which had such a short history in art.

– *When you say Modern, do you mean in the sense of originality, whoever owns the originality of one of those pictures?*

In the subjectiveness of the creative process. I of course see art much more as a chemist does; that there's nothing new in the world, it's just a re-positioning of things, it's a re-combination of things. I've now taken the stance that I am a Post-Modernist and I take this stance not only legally, because this helps me, but I believe that the Post-Modern is the return to the objective and the final dismissal of the subjective.

– *It's very refreshing to have an actual reason for being a Post-Modernist. I understand one of these law suits is from a very sad lady who took that photo of the puppies which you used in your* String of Puppies.

This was actually a man. I always thought of the *String of Puppies* as popcorn. You take a needle and thread and you put it through popcorn, and the puppies are animated and it's collaged; I put a daisy on top of their heads and I transformed them. I took something that is normally a photo and I made it into wood, gave it this spiritual quality; I coloured it with the kind of garish colours you might see in India.

– *But that could serve as an example of where you're just re-positioning the molecules. You said you were really a chemist more than a Modernist.*

This came from a postcard and anything that is a postcard puts itself in a position where it is trying to penetrate and be part of mass consciousness. If things become part of mass consciousness, how can you erase them? They are part of the vocabulary to communicate with. I don't protect myself from my environment, I let it penetrate and I let myself be victim and I, in turn, use every form of manipulation possible to victimise the public back.

– *Do you then see communication as always a process between victim and victimiser, or only in the realm of art, or in the realm of popular culture?*

I would have to say always.

– *So there's always control, there's always aggression, there's always somebody who's getting it and someone who's giving it.*

No, these words tend to be a little aggressive, but I think artists have been completely complacent, tending to support bourgeois convention, morals and economic base, instead of redefining it. So Jeff Koons is trying to redefine those conventions.

– Benjamin Buchloh, the well-known critic, once said that these were the words or these were the thoughts of a social fascist, these ideas about victim and victimiser and imposing ideas and penetrating the public. How do you respond to something like that?

I think that that's kind of pushing things a little too far, but to give an example, in the Banality show, I created a situation that was entirely democratic. The material porcelain itself was reserved for the King, and of course it has been overly democratic with Capodimonte and things; I did this not only with porcelain but with wood, and with the imagery. There was automatically a rallying cry for some Monarch to come in and take control of this overly democratic situation, which of course is a position I took.

– In other words this rallying cry resulted in the Banality group of works, where you had to take the lead.

It's put me in the position that I have a stage for my new work.

– I'm very thrilled to hear about the new work because I know a lot of people here would have been disappointed recently to hear that the movie isn't happening. So do you have anything to tell us about works that will be appearing later on in the year at the Sonnabend Gallery and Anthony D'Offay next year?

It's not that it's not happening, the movie was put on hold because the production of my work has to pay for it and I lost all my artisans that made my work, so I've had to concentrate on my exhibition. I may return to the film, even though I think that it's already played in everyone's mind. If you're not working on a movie, no PR company wants to work with you. What was your second question?

– What work is coming up?

The new work is under the banner of ' Made In Heaven'. It's a body of work that tries to show beauty in simple things, to show a close-up of life, of listening physically, visually, with all one's senses, embracing one's past. This is one's foundation to be effective in the world, to achieve one's desires. Art tends to divorce a person from their past, and this work tries to do the opposite. Taste is totally thrown out as a segregator, the sophisticated is thrown out as a segregator; they don't exist there.

– What sort of materials will we be seeing?

Glass, wood, marble and paintings.

– You had some works at the Biennale which you described as paintings which were made with this very sophisticated laser technique and were more like enormous photographs. Is this the same medium when you talk about paintings?

Most of the paintings are of myself and Ilona, my wife, who's better known as Cicciolina. They're

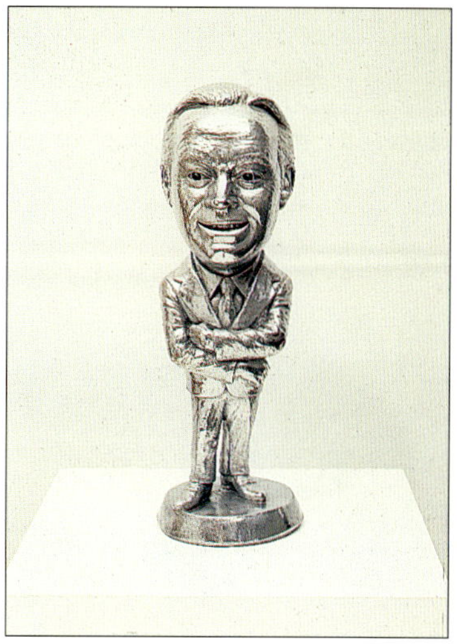

Bob Hope, *1986, stainless steel, 43x14x14cm. 'I have made many pieces that have dealt with power and what happens to art in these situations. I made a group of work called 'Statuary' in 1986 and that was a panoramic view of art and how it's been used in Western art history. On the one hand I had Louis XIV, which was a symbol of what happens when you put art into a monarch: eventually it will become reflective of their ego and decorative. On the other end of this panoramic view I had Bob Hope, and if you put art in the hands of the public, it will become reflective of mass consciousness and eventually decorative. If you put art into the hands of Jeff Koons, the same will happen, it will eventually just become decorative and a reflection of my ego.'*

paintings which deal with the interface between the subjective and the objective, they're made through a very objective manner, a machine, but they have a very subjective surface on them like romantic paintings. The whole body of work will redefine the definition of the perverse, and images which are normally looked at as distancing will seem tame and mild, and things that you would cuddle up to very closely, you will take a greater distance from.

– *That's interesting, so there are some reversals of our usual expectations to look forward to. Jeff, every now and again the word sexuality has popped up in our discussion and I wonder if you could say a bit more about that because as your reputation has broadened, I think one of the things that has kind of gelled in the public's mind is that here is an artist who shocks people with images of sexuality of one kind or another. Do you think people are missing something if they think that's all there is to it?*

If I created things to shock people I would have been destroyed a long time ago. I never create anything to shock anyone. I try to deal with myself and with the public as honestly as possible. I've tried to deal with spectacle: my *Equilibrium Tank* was purely for spectacle. I was involved with ideas of showing people something that they desire, an ultimate state of being that they haven't come into contact with.

– *What role then does sexuality play in your work, images of sexuality?*

It plays as a seducer and it also plays for my own fulfilment of sexuality. I've been able through my beliefs to satisfy my desires. Ilona and I are quite active sexually and so I'm just honest in things that I believe in. I believe in physicality.

– *Do you think that your use of that type of imagery is any different from simply an exaggerated version of images of sexuality within Pop art of the 1960s?*

I believe in taking – and I think Pop artists have done this – intellectual, cerebral ideas which are quite dry, and communicating these ideas through the genitalia. And I prefer this line of communication, I think it's more precise.

– *In the sense of making a very immediate impact?*

Not necessarily impact, but one that is an enhanced colour.

– *Wow . . . I still want to know if what you're doing is really concerned with that kind of immediate graspability that Pop art seemed to want, or if your work is merely referring to those ideas. Keith Haring T-shirts can be worn by everyone, but it seems a bit different in your case: you've been talking in an incredibly complicated way about really quite hard ideas that not everyone could be expected to get, indeed, hardly anyone.*

I have a translator who has been a teacher; she doesn't go to school and teach, but she works with me as a translator. I'm trying to use art to teach a public and help create a sense of mobility, to define life as a three-dimensional place with movement and basic political things to follow that are beneficial and very easy. I think from the womb, people need to somehow re-connect with the external, so objects take the place of the mother and the definition of the important is things that somehow can help define an external space. The end placement, of course, is to try to have as high a spiritual experience as possible and I'm trying to give a spiritual experience to people with the enhancement of my own power.

– *That's a very strong idea. In Pop art, one thing that was very rarely talked about was spirituality. In fact, there was a certain amount of glee that spirituality had finally been got rid of. Do you think that perhaps that is one very different characteristic about your own type of Pop art, the spiritual dimension? Do you see a spiritual dimension in Rosenquist and Warhol and Segal?*

Yes, I see a spiritual person trying to communicate with people, to forget about the self and to try to deal with the world and the environment past the self.

Jeff Koons, Bear and Policeman, *1988, polychromed wood, 216x109x91cm. 'These works also wanted to deal with the familiar; they didn't present themselves in a form which made the public feel guarded.'*

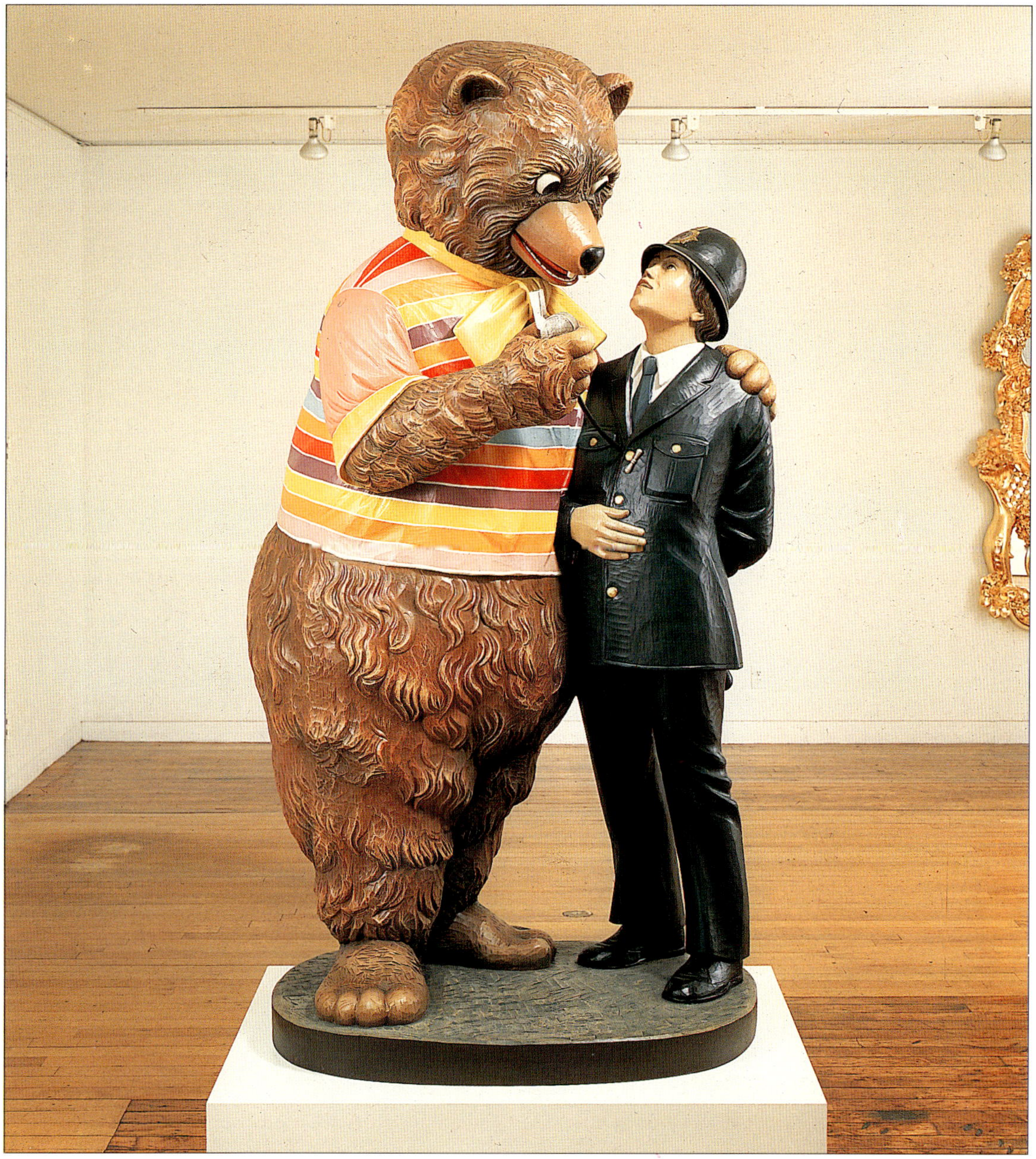

THE POP ART SYMPOSIUM
GENERAL DISCUSSION

Marco Livingstone: Having heard six artists speak today, it is remarkable how different each person's approach is, how different each personality is, and it reveals to me what I've long suspected about Pop art and about its influence: that it is a conjunction of varied movements that cannot be viewed just as one thing unless you artificially narrow it down. I'd be very interested to hear from the artists here what they think they have in common with each other especially across the generations, whether they really feel part of the same movement in any sense whatsoever. Peter Blake, can I draw you into this?

Peter Blake: Yes. I've said often that I've always felt Pop art started in three points at about the same time, that is 1954, with Richard and the Independent Group, with myself at the Royal College, and with Jasper Johns and Rauschenberg in New York. There are influences and cross-overs between us all in a way. I was enormously influenced by Jasper Johns and Rauschenberg and perhaps in turn I influenced other people. Perhaps this isn't the place to talk about my kind of discontent with the exhibition, but I do think there is an enormous over-emphasis on people like Warhol and Lichtenstein, who I always felt weren't very important artists in that I thought that the important artists were Richard, Eduardo and myself in a different way and Johns and Rauschenberg. Warhol and, I think, Lichtenstein only painted one picture and repeated it again and again with slightly different subject matters, and it seems a mistake to over-emphasise their importance in the exhibition.

Marco Livingstone: Richard Hamilton, you spoke rather glowingly this morning about Warhol, and it seems to me that for the younger artists he remains the most important example and a very strong presence that is difficult to ignore. How do you feel from your perspective about Warhol's position today?

Richard Hamilton: I think he is enormously important. I'm not sure that he only did one picture; I think his ideas were continuing and there is a development throughout his whole career. But the one thing I find odd about exhibitions such as this is that European and British art in particular looks rather small-scale, compared with this gigantic heavyweight American production, and in the catalogues it's all squeezed down to the same size and you begin to see that they do have equivalencies. I like catalogues much more, because it gives us a better chance to compete!

Constance Glenn: I was thinking about what both Richard and Peter were saying. In America we don't think of you all as Pop artists, and Ashley used an interesting word, 'permission'. In the United States we refer to Johns and Rauschenberg as having given permission for a variety of kinds of art, a variety of attitudes and a variety of expressions and we think of both of you that way as well. Not as that generation of college kids born in the mid 30s who were, at least in the United States, hard-core Pop artists. I definitely think of you and Peter and Jasper and Bob as the people who made the breakthrough and who gave the permission to the Pop art generation.

OVERLEAF: The Pop Art Show, Royal Academy, London, (left to right) Peter Blake, Siriol, She-Devil of Naked Madness, *1957,* Toy Shop, *1962,* Kim Novak Wall, *1959,* Bo Diddley, *1963; Tom Wesselman,* Bathroom Collage #2, *1963; Richard Hamilton,* Glorious Techniculture, *1961-64 (photo Stephen White)*

Richard Hamilton: The main thing about the period for me, and it is very well represented in the exhibition, was that there was a great deal of intermingling. Fluxus was something that emerged in Darmstadt and there were connections with Vienna and 'happenings'; they were simultaneous.

Constance Glenn: I think that Yves Klein brought that same kind of permission in France as well. He also had quite a bit of influence in America.

Richard Hamilton: Yves Klein was very popular. He did a lecture at the ICA in the 60s which was a tremendous pop-cabaret phenomenon. What was marvellous about it was the permissiveness between the artists – everyone enjoyed each other's company. It was an international phenomenon and there wasn't any feeling that people were excluded from this club. There was a very general acceptance which meant that you could be very well placed with Beuys, Marcel Broodthaers, Jasper Johns, Rauschenberg, Morris. There were all these very different personalities; I did not see them as a group, I saw them as individuals. What they had in common was an acceptance, an openness to the work of other people. That generosity was a main characteristic and it appears in the exhibition.

Richard Cork: The difference in temperature between the first room and the second room is very instructive. I was surprised by how raw a lot of the work in the first room still looks, especially the Rauschenbergs and the early Dines. Those are very tough things, and I was surprised by their strong relationship to Abstract Expressionism. When you enter the second room you are into a different world. It's much tighter, it is much more finished, polished, it's a different sensibility, even though there are all these fascinating connections. Peter Blake's wall introduces you to a very personal world indeed. Unlike anybody else's it has its own flavour, its own mood and the same with your wall, Richard. It's incredibly precise and carefully worked compared with a lot of work in the first room.

Peter Blake: I think the thing that worries me is exactly what you've said, Richard, about that particular selection of work. I did talk to Marco and I did have a chance to adjust it. Because I did believe in Marco's book so much and because for the first time ever I was given some credit for what I did in Pop art, I think I was in a kind of rosy glow when I read that list and didn't want to grumble yet again. But I think they look quite different as pictures on the wall. By a sad coincidence, they are all rather dark pictures. The *Kim Novak Wall*, which is the one representation of that group of pictures, is the one black picture, and the *Bo Diddley* also happens to be a dark picture, and I would criticise myself if I saw that show.

Marco Livingstone: There are three great pictures by Jasper Johns and I don't think the colour makes any difference, I think they come over very strongly; we have also got the smallest map ever made and I think the idea is still very powerful.

Peter Blake: But although I say it myself, they look British, they look tiny, they look parochial, they look things that I wouldn't want them to look. I am not saying that I should have had more pictures in,

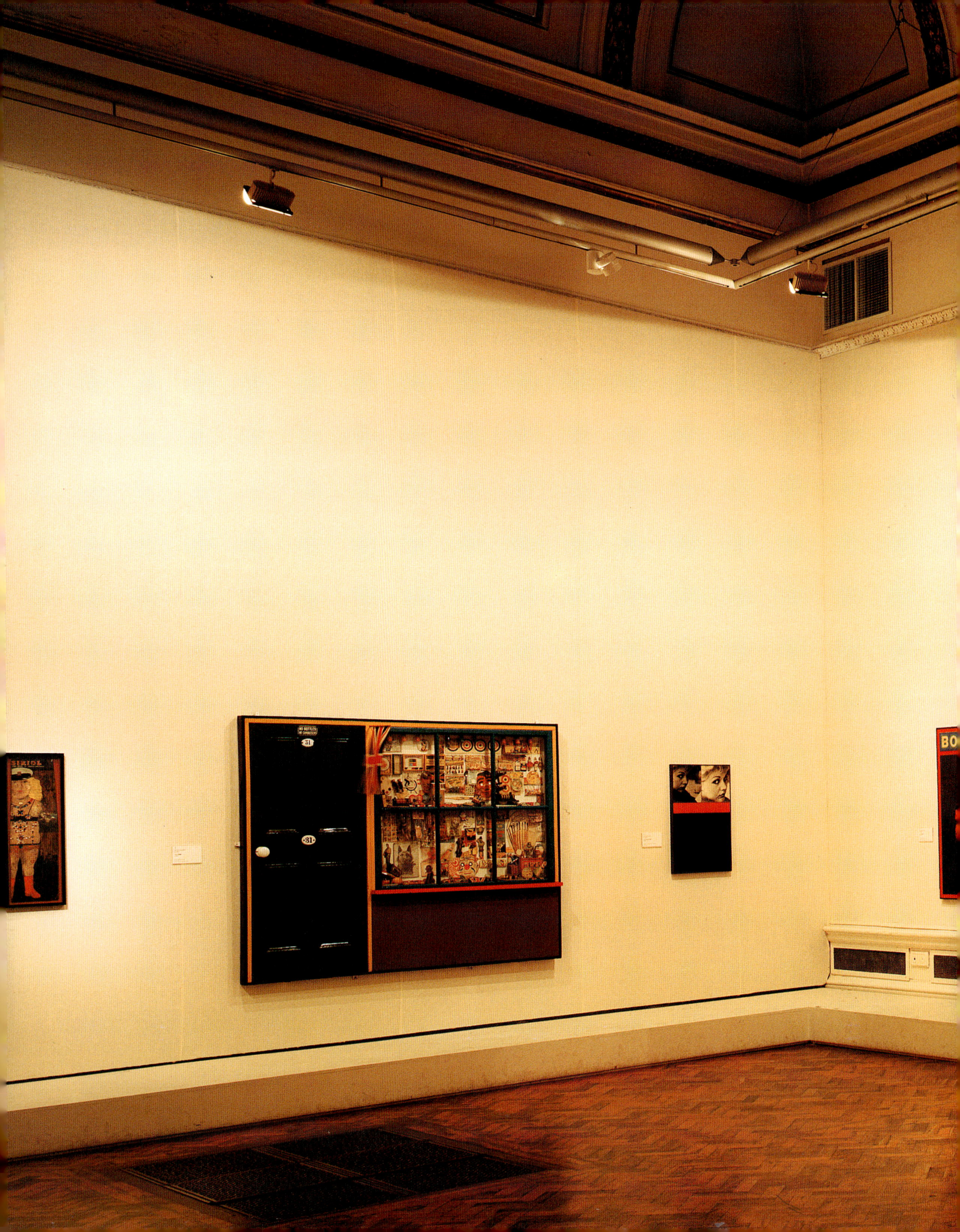
SIRIOL

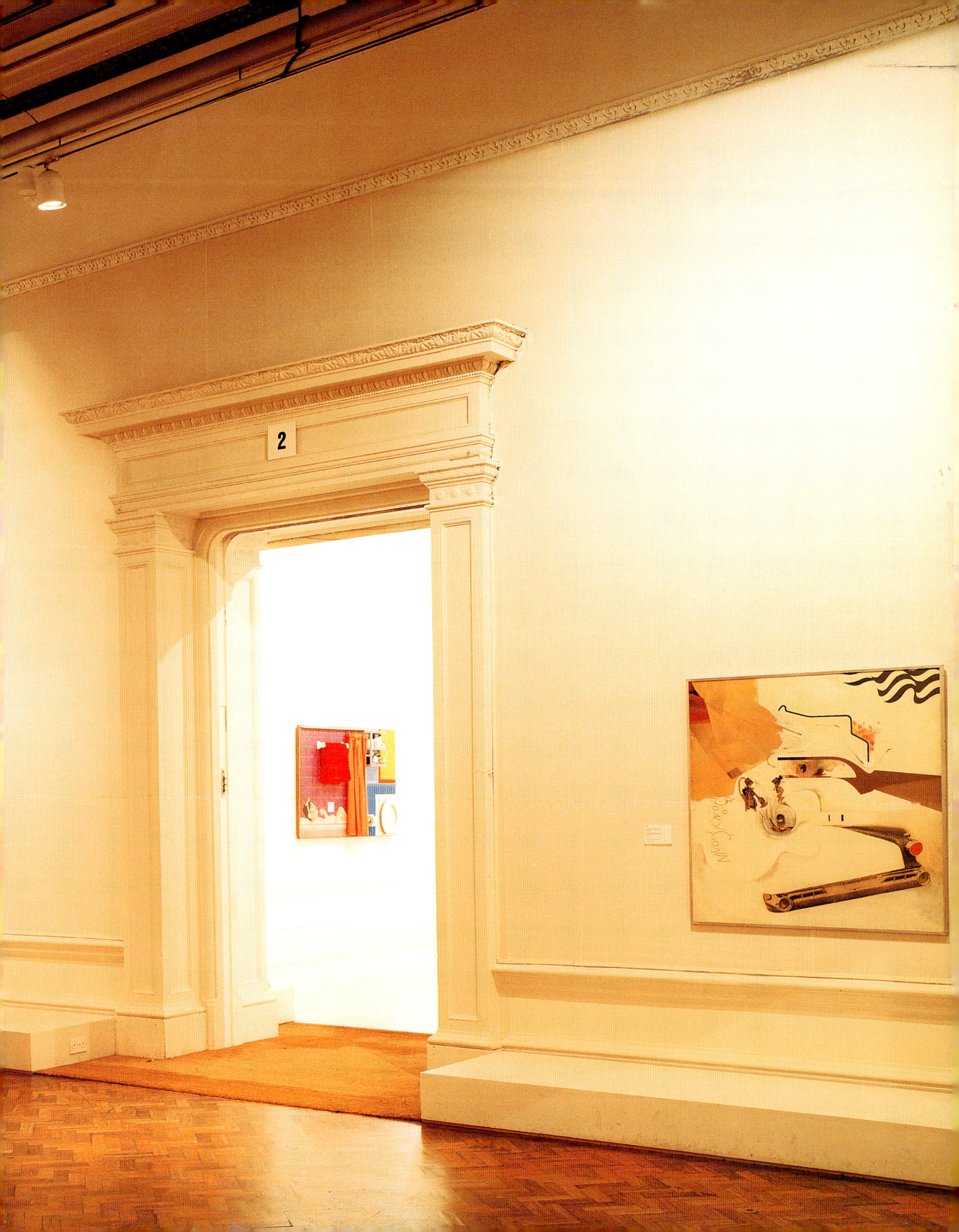
2

but there are other pictures like the *Self-Portrait*, there are pictures like *Got A Girl,* the Beatles picture, *Girls with their Hero,* things like *The Locker.* The curious thing was seeing Dan Cameron's slides of a whole selection of new people not shown at the Serpentine. I felt that I had done all those pictures, like making a locker, making doors, shelves, all kinds of things that I saw in that work. Anyone coming to this exhibition wouldn't get that feeling, you would get a feeling of being very British and very parochial.

Marco Livingstone: I have been as surprised as anyone to see how everything looks together. I have been, as you know, researching the subject since the mid 70s when I was a student and especially doing everything that I can to bring the British case to the public. What amazed me when I saw everything together was to see how absolutely different the work is from one side of the Atlantic to the other: it has the same name but the purposes were very different, the scale is different, the speed with which one experiences the work is different. The Warhols and the Lichtensteins are very intense in their immediate impact, very bold, they excluded a lot from their work deliberately for that purpose and what you're doing is very different. I do not know how it feels to someone coming across the work for the first time. I think people in this country have obviously seen your work quite thoroughly in the past. There was a very big retrospective at the Tate a few years ago. In this kind of exhibition it is rather pointless and confusing to present a whole series of one-man shows that do not make any sense together. I think that the British come over quite strongly, but it is a different sort of art – it is much more intimate, much more personal; your attitude in your work is very different from most of what we have heard today. The kind of affectionate attitude towards popular culture is very different from the much more detached – and what some people might call cynical – view of someone like Jeff Koons. I think people recognise that, moving from room to room, and some people actually prefer your work to a 45-foot Rosenquist even though the immediate impact of the scale is obviously going to be very powerful.

Richard Hamilton: There is one major distinction between American work and British work and that is that the British work has always had a very bad press. A recent exhibition of mine was criticised by Sarah Kent, who may have an answer to this, and she ended by saying, 'How sad, how British'. This is the worst criticism you could make of any artist, this is real cut-throat stuff and it has persisted for a very long time.

Constance Glenn: You have enjoyed enormous popularity in America, a good press.

Richard Cork: I was going to say that what we live with is British criticism.

Constance Glenn: I doubt that any of us are happy with our criticism.

Richard Cork: I think actually that one of the fascinating differences between the Americans and the Brits is how densely packed the Brits are, there is so much going on in them. There are so many references, so many allusions, so many playful little additions in the corners, they are almost inexhaustible. You could return to them again and again and never really get to the end of what they are referring to. Then you turn the corner into the first big white gallery and there is a sort of Pop art which is stripped bare and says to you, look at the strip-cartoon, look at the advert, look at the

Campbell's soup can and nothing else, that's all we are going to give you. The difference between those two sensibilities is enormous.

OVERLEAF: The Pop Art Show, Royal Academy, London, (left to right) Ed Ruscha, The Los Angeles County Museum of Art on Fire, *1965-68,* Talk about Space, *1963; Mel Ramos,* Miss Cushion Air (Miss Firestone), *1965; Edward Kienholz,* John Doe, *1959,* Walter Hopps, Hopps, Hopps, *1959; David Hockney,* A Bigger Splash, *1967; Mel Ramos,* Batmobile, *1962 (photo Stephen White)*

Constance Glenn: But Jim thought there was a great difference between the source material too. He felt the whole Times Square American advertising day-glo colour was so extreme that the mere nature of the sources the American Pop artists were working from were quite different from the sources which the British and the continental European Pop artists were working from. He felt that the fast recognition, large-scale, extreme colour contrast of the American work was purely a result of the environment.

Marco Livingstone: I think really the test of all the work in the exhibition is whether it is true to its own culture. I think for British art to try to look like the American wouldn't have worked, it was created in a different situation. It was quite right that your work should have a different feel, a different quality, surface, scale. Perhaps people will get a greater impact from the larger work, going around the exhibition for the first time, but because your pictures are small, they encourage a closer scrutiny. I think one often experiences works by Warhol from a great distance and never looks at their surface. You see the image and you think that's it and perhaps it doesn't get as close a look as it should.

Peter Blake: I got a slight feeling of footnote. You went into those first two rooms and in a way they were kind of historic rooms. They had dark wooden floors, the lighting was much lower. They felt slightly colder than the other rooms, you looked around at the early history of Pop art and it was as if you could then put that away and get on with the exhibition.

Norman Rosenthal: I thought those were the two most powerful rooms just because they are in a sense a poorer, more democratic art. One of the things we tried to do in the exhibition was to illustrate the move from an art which was not of the rich galleries and for rich people, but was made out of an environment of happenings, performances, discussions and a kind of popular sensibility, particularly in your case, to a kind of art that has a great deal to do with rich galleries. That is why we brought in the idea of the white floors, so that one can read these things in two different ways. A lot of people were impressed by the freshness and originality of the first two rooms. I think, Peter, you misunderstand how a lot of people react to this exhibition. I think that what is extraordinary about your contribution and that of Jasper Johns and Rauschenberg at the beginning was that you brought incredible new impulses to art which are still being transformed by artists today. But I mean 30 years ago there were no Walkmans, televisions were black and white, the world was a different place, New York was different to London and I think all these things were reflected in the exhibition. We have got to try and understand the affinities between the work that was going on in London and the work that was going on in New York and the work that was going on in Europe. Lawrence Alloway called it Pop art but it could have been called New Realism, or Neo-Dada. Pop was a good word, a brilliant journalistic device like Impressionism. I don't know if Alloway meant it in a totally positive sense, maybe the word Pop was almost used cynically, but it stuck. Perhaps it was almost an accident that it was called Pop art. When you painted your early pictures did you know you were a Pop artist, using the word in that sense?

Peter Blake: No, of course I didn't. I was actually present when Lawrence Alloway coined the

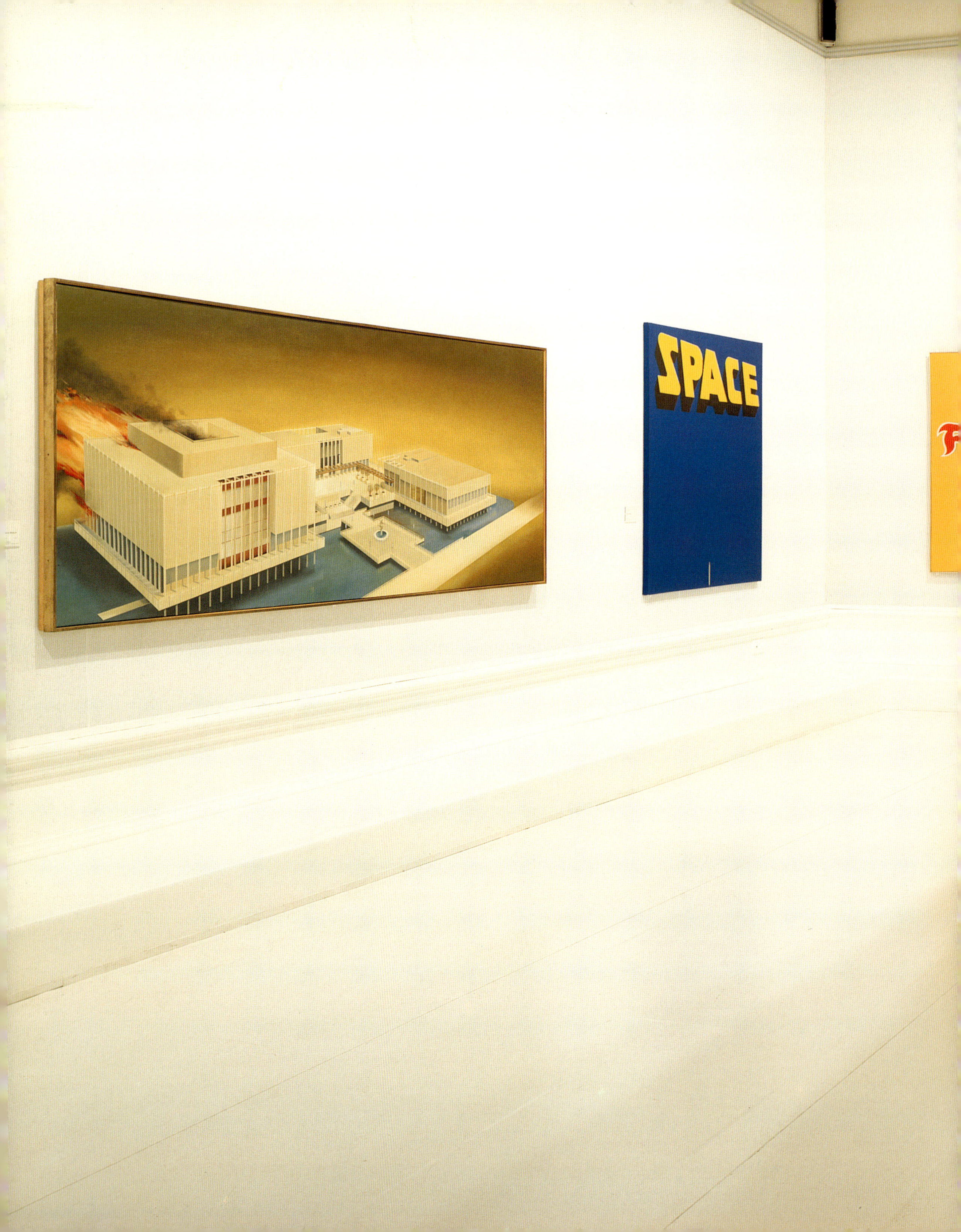
SPACE

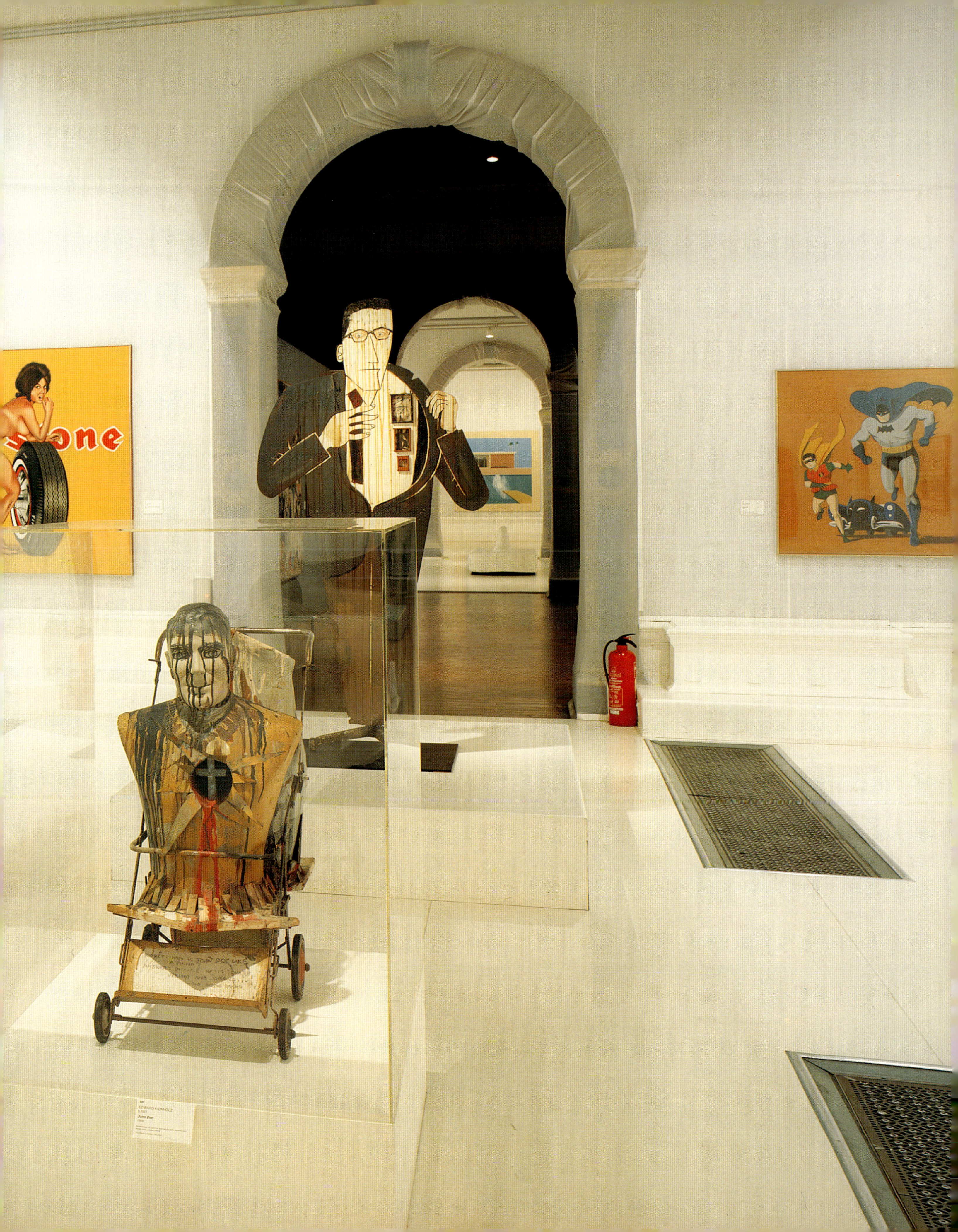
EDWARD KIENHOLZ
John Doe

phrase Pop art. It was a serious conversation and we were talking about the possibility of making an art that was the equivalent of, say, pop music to classical music.

Norman Rosenthal: But Pop art and pop music are not the same thing. The revelation of the exhibition for me was it is not as if everybody signed a manifesto for all time and stuck to it. It's a very broad umbrella. I would like to know from Richard when he first heard the word Pop and suddenly discovered he was a Pop artist? Did the word suddenly become so current that he couldn't get away from it?

Richard Hamilton: I don't think Lawrence Alloway did invent the idea of Pop art. He certainly used the word pop as we all did to refer to popular culture, that is the work of professionals for large numbers of people in Hollywood, the music industry and so on. The word pop was used quite self-consciously to distinguish it from the popular arts, which meant painting barges and that sort of thing, so we knew what we were talking about. It wasn't until there was an exhibition that other critics started calling it Pop art because they made the mistake of thinking that Lawrence Alloway had labelled it that. I think that Lawrence was quite happy to accept the attribution, but I didn't think it was a serious thing that Lawrence labelled it Pop art. In fact his interests didn't lie in that direction at all. The exhibitions he was putting on at the time were hard-edged abstractionist and Situationist exhibitions. If you look at the history, you will see that he was completely immersed in the influence on Britain of Ellsworth Kelly, and it wasn't until he went to America that he realised Pop art existed.

Marco Livingstone: I think that in a way Alloway never really understood British Pop art.

Richard Hamilton: We didn't look at each other's art until there was an uncomfortable feeling about it. Lawrence was a close friend and spent at least one evening a month at my house, as I did at his, and we never discussed my work. After four of five years of this I had to say to him on the stairs at the ICA, 'Lawrence, what do you think of my paintings?' He said 'I think they are stupid!' So I am perfectly well aware that he didn't invent Pop art or the term.

Constance Glenn: You know perhaps the first nine shows did not include the word Pop. The titles were 'The New Realists', 'Six Painters and the Object'.

Richard Hamilton: Lawrence invited me to contribute to the first show he did in America, which was a show of British drawings and I said I would like to show the little collage and he said 'Oh, we don't want that, we want drawings!' It was the first show he put on as curator of the Guggenheim.

Richard Cork: Richard, who do you think coined the term Pop art, then?

Richard Hamilton: I think it was a misunderstanding. British critics had heard this word used by Alloway in a different context and they applied it to these things they thought were concerned with art. They thought that Lawrence had invented the word, but it was a very nice mistake, I'm very glad it happened.

Peter Blake: Well I have told the story, perhaps it didn't happen like that, perhaps I just want to think it did. But as I remember it, we were having a conversation about the art I was making – it was possibly about the show at the ICA in 1958 or 1960 – and we were talking about the possibility of my making an art that was the equivalent of pop music and would appeal to the people who listen to it. I was trying to make pictures that a 16-year-old Elvis Presley fan would read in the same way that she would listen to a record. And I failed to do this because the imagery didn't work, but I still think that the phrase Pop art came out of that conversation.

OVERLEAF: The Pop Art Show, Royal Academy, London, (clockwise) Andy Warhol, 80 2-Dollar Bills, Front and Rear, *1962,* Blue Liz as Cleopatra, *1963,* Early Colored Liz, *1963,* Marilyn, *1964,* White Car Crash, 19 times, *1963; Robert Rauschenberg,* Spot, *1963; Claes Oldenburg,* Plate of Meat, *1961,* US Flag Fragment, *1961,* Sewing Machine, *1961; Andy Warhol,* Boxes, *1964 (photo Stephen White)*

Richard Hamilton: I don't remember critics using the term Pop art in relation to fine art until the Arthur Jefferies exhibition in around 1961. That was the term used by the critics of that exhibition.

Marco Livingstone: Alloway wrote the introduction to the Young Contemporaries catalogue in 1961 at which Hockney and Kitaj and Boshier were shown. He did not use the term, I think he conspicuously avoided it, I don't think he thought about it in relation to the art either.

Richard Cork: Can I raise a point that exhibitions by their very nature can't deal with, which came out very strongly this morning? In all the contributions this morning, the artists talked about cross-fertilisation and how important this was to their work. I hadn't realised this so strongly before. Richard, you talked about the Independent Group and all those ideas and the book reading, and then the Americans talked about 'happenings' and composers and dance. The 'compost' which helped to create Pop was multifarious in that way and I suppose an exhibition cannot hope to deal with that properly.

Peter Blake: I felt very disjointed from the talk this afternoon. This morning seemed to be on an intelligent level, especially Richard talking to Richard, which I enjoyed enormously. But this afternoon I got the feeling that Jeff Koons was like Tiny Tim, and I couldn't get away from it. He simply wasn't telling the truth; he was making up answers all along and saying what he thought ought to be said; and with Ashley Bickerton the same thing happened, the interviewer suddenly sounded like Philip Hodson, the Radio Doctor, with Ashley Bickerton as his patient. It was a different world, just as Jeff Koons was brash, Ashley Bickerton was artificially shy and it felt very odd.

Marco Livingstone: I did not get the feeling that Ashley Bickerton was artificially shy. I just thought he was very nervous to have to defend his work straight after a performance like Jeff Koons'.

Peter Blake: It all felt rather like acting.

Constance Glenn: It didn't look greatly different to me from the film maker's cinematic in New York in 1962. I found great concordances in the personality and the modes of expression, and a lot of the American Pop artists say that if American Pop did anything, it made it possible to say 'anything goes'. I think this afternoon we are seeing the result of that.

Peter Blake: There is no truth; 'anything goes' almost implies that.

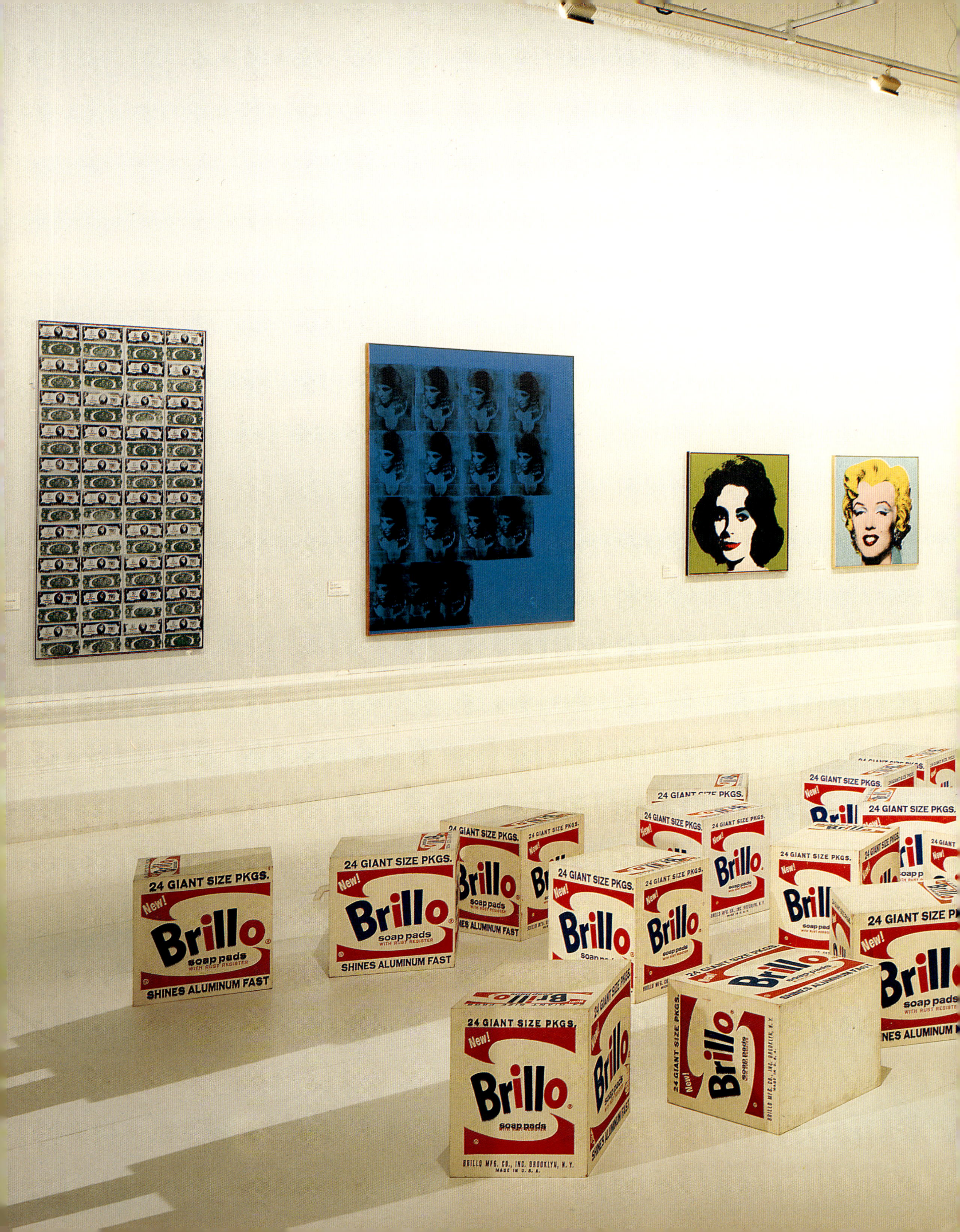

24 GIANT SIZE PKGS.
New!
Brillo
soap pads
WITH RUST RESISTER
SHINES ALUMINUM FAST
BRILLO MFG. CO., INC. BROOKLYN, N.Y.
MADE IN U.S.A.

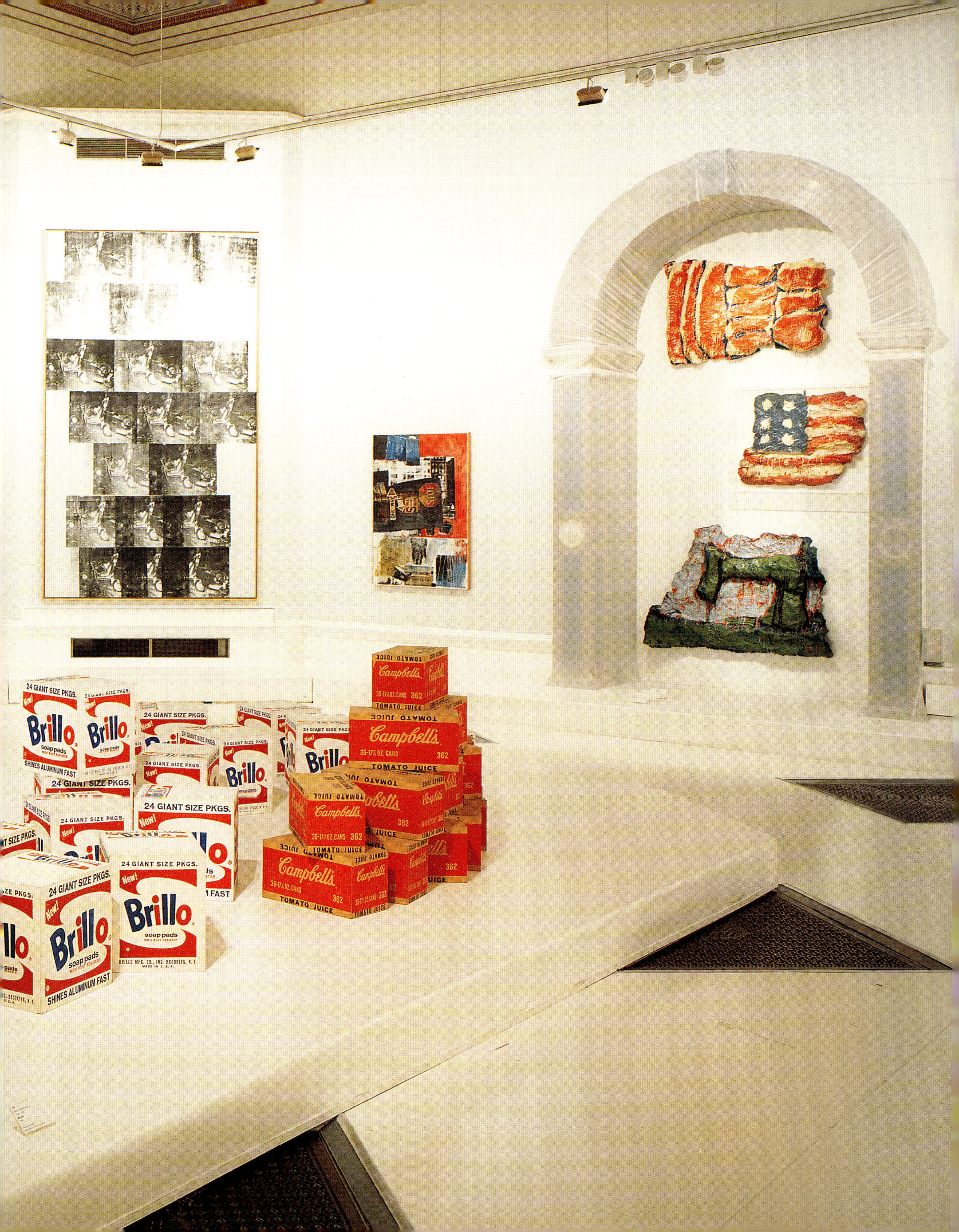
24 GIANT SIZE PKGS.
New!
Brillo
soap pads
SHINES ALUMINUM FAST
BRILLO MFG. CO., INC. BROOKLYN, N.Y.
Campbell's
36-17½ OZ. CANS 362
TOMATO JUICE

Constance Glenn: The phrase 'anything goes' was Rosenquist's. He said there was a sense in American Pop art of joy and light-heartedness that you certainly don't find so much in the inheritors. But it was a world of anything goes, anything can be used to make art, it's the street, the city scene, it's street refuse; I can pick up elements for a collage out of the gutter. Jim always says that he feels that period of Pop art was unfinished.

Norman Rosenthal: I think it is quite wrong to feel that all interesting art today can be put under the umbrella of Neo-Pop. It is also informed by a lot of other things that have happened in the meantime. Because we have the Pop art exhibition at the Royal Academy and the legacy of Pop at the Serpentine, that is a message that could easily become confused.

Constance Glenn: Both Bickerton and Koons, I think, made it quite clear that they come out of a very chequered background that includes Pop art but the Cal Arts brand of conceptualism is easily as major an influence in both of these artists.

Richard Cork: I think one of the great strengths of the Academy show is that unlike a lot of historical exhibitions which one goes to see, you don't get any sense of a movement that is somewhat sealed off in time. It is a question of timing. If this show had been held ten years ago it would have had a very different feel. You would have thought you were dealing with a sort of historical phenomenon that was somehow shut away and which didn't bear much on the concerns of young artists. But I think the timing is perfect for this show, and you get the feeling going round the Royal Academy show that it is still going on, that it is still to be resolved.

Norman Rosenthal: Pop is an impulse that will never go away but I think it is quite wrong to suggest that the subjective will never come back, and that there is no room for the subjective or for painting. Pop art brought incredible impulses that will never go away as did Cubism and as did Surrealism, as did Dada and many other movements.

Marco Livingstone: I was surprised, Richard, to hear Jeff Koons talk about Pop art as Post-Modernist, and I know other people have this view. I still see it as very much to do with Modernism.

Richard Hamilton: I don't know. I was once sitting in Yale with a group of academics and somebody asked me how it feels to be responsible for Post-Modernism! I haven't seen the Serpentine show but I know something of that work as I've seen it in Paris and at the Saatchi gallery, and it seems odd to me that in spite of the extraordinary sophistication of the presentation of Jeff Koons and Ashley Bickerton this afternoon, there is a certain naivety through their work and their thinking. Naive in that they do not seem to have any real historical sense. How do they react when they see Clive Barker's *Van Gogh Chair*? It seems that the blown up bunnies could have been done by Clive Barker 30 years ago. Do they feel guilty about it or do they say, well that's a primitive of what we are doing?

Richard Cork: One thing I thought was missing from the show and I only realised it this morning when Richard was talking about the first time he saw the sheer size of some of Warhol's work; in a curious way I missed that in the show, the hugeness of early Warhol, the vastness of early Rosenquist.

I suppose it is to do with problems of borrowing and displaying?

Marco Livingstone: We decided to show the scale of Rosenquist with later work so that you see the stylistic development, but also an example of that huge bill-board scale that really only happened at that point. The first really huge painting was 1980.

Constance Glenn: You must remember the pictures have shrunk since 1962. Those pictures seemed so big when they were first painted because they were put out in a world of comic strips and newspapers, they were taken almost immediately into ordinary houses with eight-foot ceilings. They do not look huge in the Royal Academy, they do not carry that sense of bigness that they carried when they were new.

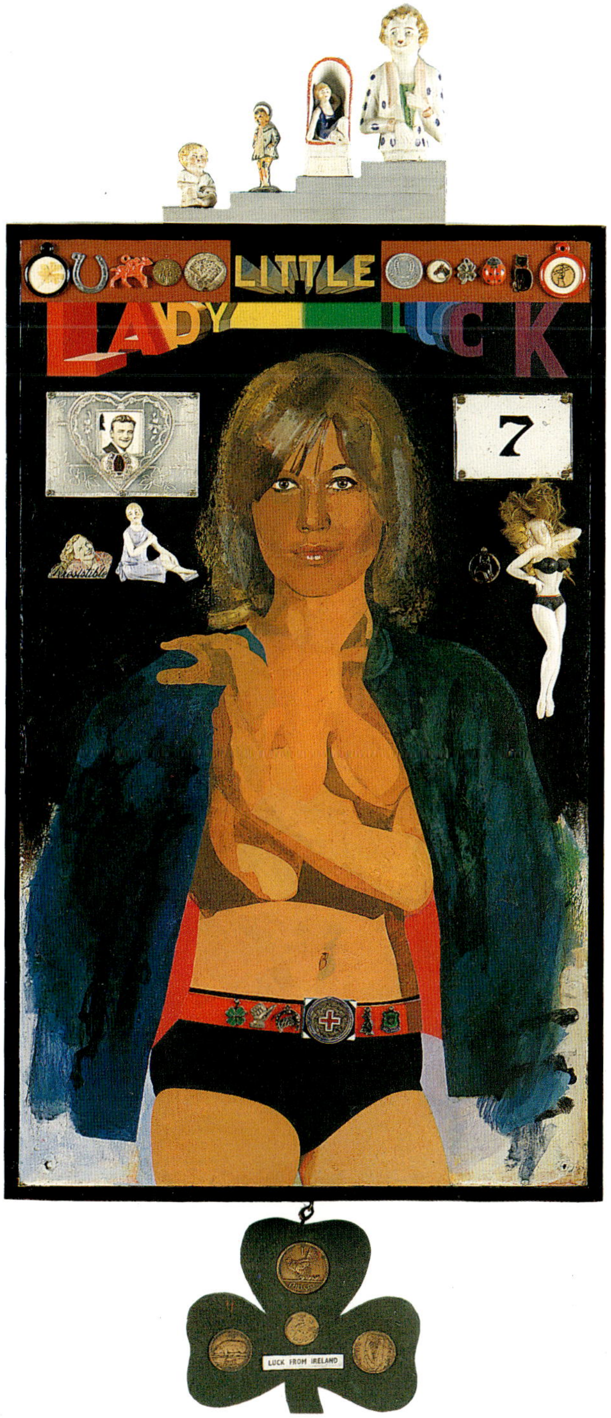

Peter Blake, Little Lady Luck, *1965, cryla and collage on hardboard, 72x35cm*

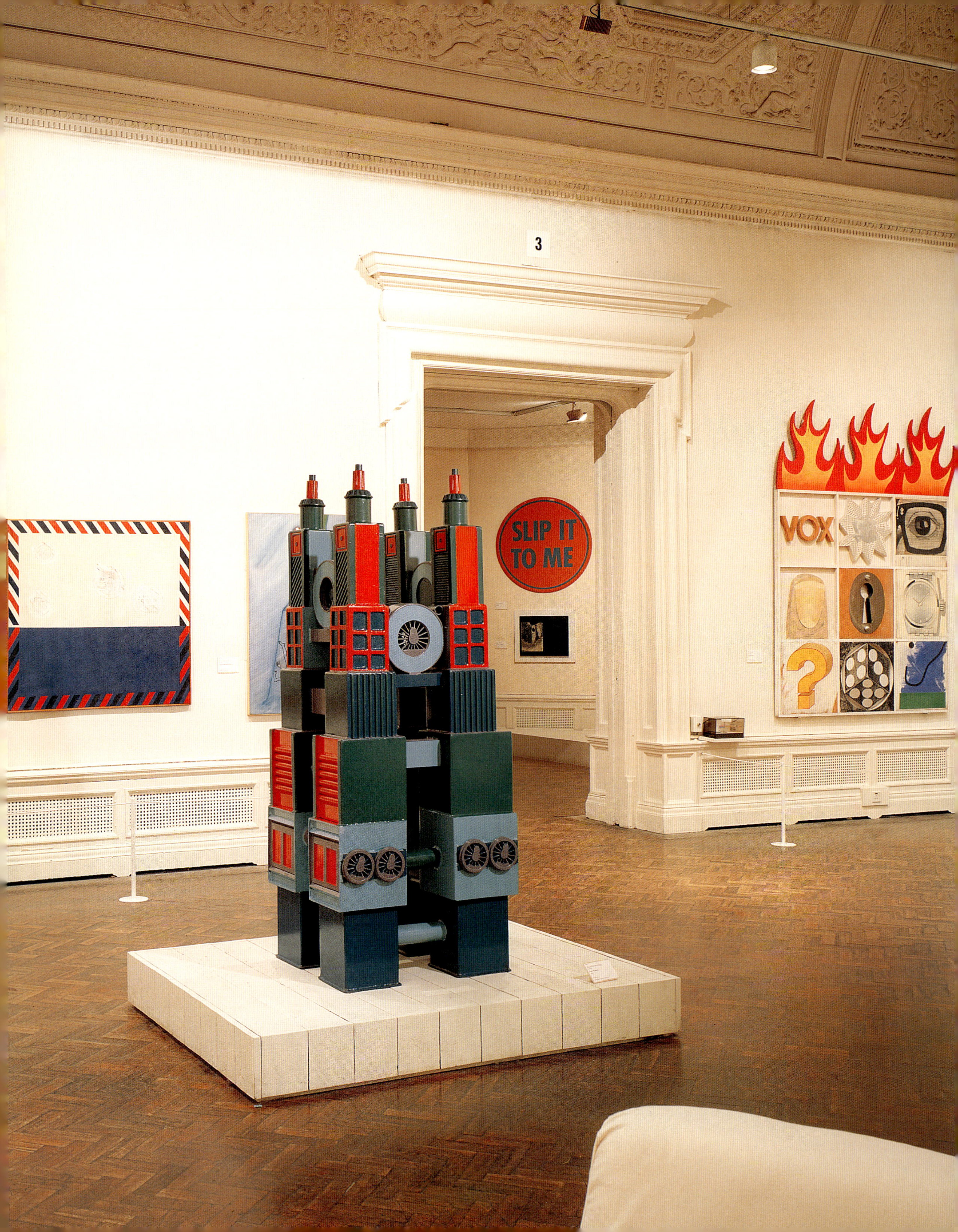
3
SLIP IT
TO ME
VOX

MICHAEL COMPTON

POP ART IN BRITAIN

The Pop Art Show, Royal Academy, London, (left to right) Derek Boshier, Airmail Letter, *1961; Eduardo Paolozzi,* Four Towers, *1962; Richard Hamilton,* Epiphany, *1964; Clive Barker,* Two Palettes for Jim Dine, *1964; Joe Tilson,* Nine Elements, *1963 (photo Stephen White)*

The artists, works of art and ideas that together made up the phenomenon of Pop art[1] in Britain have been described again and again during the last 30 years; art historical antecedents and social motives have been picked out and discussed. Contemporary opinion, if it did not see Pop art simply as a debasement of art, mostly inclined to one of two positions. One group saw it as genuinely populist or anti-authoritarian, the other deemed it complicit in the art market (and by implication in capitalism), whether cynically or naively so. Since then, the critical picture of Pop has hardly changed, even though more and more detail has been filled in, above all by Marco Livingstone. One of the reasons for this stability is that Pop's populist 'theory' was established in advance by a combination of artists and art critics or historians. The art, when it emerged, was identified in relation to this. A second reason is that those movements which followed and drew on aspects of Pop art have stuck to the 'complicit' critique so as to represent themselves as progressive by contrast.

Pop art in Britain appeared in two main phases: the first included several experienced artists, working through a series of transitions, the other a quick bloom of young artists for whom Pop was their first mature voice or theme. The first hints of Pop can be found in the rising interest taken in non-elite (low-brow) sub-cultures, which flourish everywhere and always.[2] This interest can be seen among writers who were mainly concerned with cultures to which they did not belong and by some artists and art students who were equally concerned with those to which they did belong or to which they had access. The enthusiastically painted breakfast tables of John Bratby, for example, were an avowal of such belonging. In the mid 50s the pages of *Ark* magazine, the journal of the Royal College of Art then edited by Roger Coleman, included written and pictorial accounts of, for example, the musical sub-cultures to which many students and artists subscribed, but representations of it were in the picturesque styles typical of contemporary book illustration. Comics were commented on, reproduced and pastiched but they, too, were treated merely as subjects. Gradually, the consciousness of participating by exchange of signs became stronger. The popularisation of anthropology, archaeology, information theory and even art history, provided conceptual means for picking out and evaluating cases. These disciplines also constituted sub-cultures of their own, of which one might gain associate membership by reading articles or books and adopting some of their jargon. The scientific or sociological flavour of much of the discussion had a long history in the self-education movements of the British working class and was distinct from the aestheticised, mandarin political philosophy that played a similar role in continental Europe.

In visual art, the principal focus of the changing viewpoint was the Institute of Contemporary Arts in London. The first major manifestation of the new sensibility was the exhibition '140,000 Years of Modern Art', 1948, in which images from all periods and cultures were presented as being of their own time and place, but nevertheless as art, available to artists as sources of pictorial language and validating the anti-academic traditions of modern art. The exhibitions 'Growth and Form' (ICA 1951), 'Parallel of Life and Art' (ICA 1953) and 'Man, Machine and Motion' (Newcastle University, ICA and

Leeds City Art Gallery 1955-56), were anthologies of imagery drawn from a wider variety of sources including much that was scientific, technological or commercial. The catalogue of 'Man, Machine and Motion' contains an introduction by Lawrence Gowing and Richard Hamilton, emphasising the fabulous and aesthetic aspect of engineering products and of technical illustration. But the comments on the images by Reyner Banham mark a change of direction. He notes sources and social functions of stylistic features and techniques of representation. Semiotics had appeared in tandem with art history. The difference in character and tone between his comments on advertising and motor styling and the nearly contemporary essays of Roland Barthes is marked. Banham assumes a public more or less classless and self selecting, with a high degree of freedom and control (through knowledge and choice) of the media they consume, whereas Barthes imagines a (malignant) bourgeoisie in control of all mythologising language. Banham: 'The sources of the stylists' and ad-men's precision and sensitivity is the continuous testing of the public response to 'dream-car' projects which dramatise improvements and developments which could be built into production models.' Barthes: '. . . the car on show is explored with an intense, amorous studiousness . . . The object [Citroën DS = Déesse = Goddess] is totally prostituted, appropriated: originating from the heaven of *Metropolis*, the Goddess is in a quarter of an hour mediatised, actualising through this exorcism the very essence of petit-bourgeois advancement.'[3] Banham writes in the language of what he writes about, Barthes in that of the literary intellectual. Both understood the advertiser's and stylist's device of associating the product with the symbols rather than the actuality of sex, power etc, but Barthes seems to suppose that only the intellectual (himself) understands this and must oppose it. Blinded by his own theorising, he imagines that working-class people have a single impoverished language. Banham imagines the contrary and the Pop artists were to demonstrate it in their art.

The cool wit and technical allusions of the ICA culture of this time were fostered at the meetings of the Independent Group within it. Its members met during 1952-55 to discuss papers and presentations in which, for example, science, science fiction and art were treated on an equal basis. The sensibility was less that of Surrealism than that of Purism and Modernist architecture; Ozenfant's *Foundations of Modern Art*, which finds and celebrates order throughout nature and culture, was much cited. In the discussions, the analytic frameworks of anthropology might be applied to art, or those of art-historical iconography to the covers of science fiction magazines. It is not recorded whether any of the ideas coming from art were useful to scientists or engineers but some of those that went the other way were suggestive. For example it was recognised that structures in outer space would not have to have the integrated envelopes of those forcing themselves through air or water at high speed, or those that may need to be kept clean or be interchangeable elements in an office or kitchen. They could, therefore, be additive in structure, made up of diverse modules, bolted together or hung on a framework, as the pods of the imaginative architecture of Archigram were to be. The same principle could be applied to the aggregation of units of meaning, whether iconographic or stylistic. An analogy to this conception was found in Marshall MacLuhan's *The Mechanical Bride*, 1951. This was the most commonly read text dealing with the media environment and is in fact introduced by a phrase saying that it may be read in any order. The final exhibition that may be associated with the culture of the Independent Group was 'This is Tomorrow' at the Whitechapel Gallery, 1956. It comprised a set of collaborative environments, which effectively anthologised the interests of the group. The structures, whether architectural, sculptural, pictorial or semiotic, tended to the non-hierarchical, non-Euclidean and associative. The poster artwork by Richard Hamilton, *Just what is it that makes today's homes so different, so appealing?* exemplifies this character.

Few works of art can be associated precisely with the ideas expressed at the Independent Group, but among them *$he* and *Hommage à Chrysler Corp.* by Richard Hamilton, as well as *Just what is it. . .*, are the core and apogee of this phase of Pop art. They are additive and deploy a range of images (or rather fragments of images) and styles, drawn from those used to give meaning (desirability) to consumer durables, or identity to works of art. They illustrate the exchange of techniques between high and low art and demonstrate the possibility of learning their codes. The paintings themselves remain unequivocally high art. Their structure retains elements of perspective and is strongly thematic, so that, although additive, it is distinct from most Cubist or Dada collage. In a lecture given at Newcastle University and the ICA in 1959, 'Persuading Image',[4] Hamilton, as a life-long socialist, shows a complete lack of naivety about the advertiser's function in controlling the consumer so as to create a market for a constantly and arbitrarily changing product, but he argues that this is necessary to accelerate real development, significant choice and affordability. Soon after, in a lecture to the National Union of Teachers, 'Popular Culture and Personal Responsibility', he argued that 'in an ideal culture . . . awareness of its condition is universal . . . [and] each of its members accepts the convenience of different values for different groups.'[5] His own work as a fine artist may be considered an education in these propositions. It was a sort of deconstruction or demystification, but one flavoured with wit rather than moralising.

The collaged works of McHale and the bronze sculptures of Paolozzi in the late 50s reassembled imagery from technical and commercial sources into humanoid monsters, themselves a favourite theme in the iconography of comics, science fiction and movies, but also of Surrealism. This type of work assumes not only the artist's freedom to reconstruct myth but a public capable of seeing what has been done, and bringing to it responses educated by familiarity with its references. The assumption is equivalent to that required by a literature underpinned by classical and historical references. Paolozzi also made simple collages of images of all sorts that interested him. The arrangements leave much of the material relatively intact and their combination is witty rather than mordantly satirical or tragic.

Peter Blake's art from the same period exhibits a very different range of myth-making and association. Scientific and technological references are missing and those to the highly industrialised American media less evident. Where these do appear, they are accorded no special status, they may be toys or ornaments and are thoroughly anglicised. He asserts control by dealing precisely and only with what he wants and often takes personal possession of diverse commercially produced imagery by repainting it rather than by collage. In his early works, comics and badges and the other objects of his affection appear as still-life, even if they threaten to take over the whole picture. His painting style is very coherent, leaving few of the gaps that in contemporary artists imply a distance between the artist and his material or any kind of irony. It is not cool, as Hamilton's, but warm, even sentimental.

The suspicion and hostility shown by critics towards vulgar art and towards the industrialised media of communication, was commonly based on the assumption of its alien, engulfing power. This feeling is commonly expressed in Continental European art, for example that of Polke, but in England it was in itself a provocation to artists to show that they could make use of the material without danger to themselves. The opinion of the American critic Dwight McDonald that the gap between high and low culture reflects a class difference and that the 'fuzziness of class distinctions in America, leading to competition and merging between the two cultures, is bewildering and demoralising,'[6] may have made

American sources even more seductive. On the other hand, the American writer David Lerner, in *The Human Meaning of the Social Sciences*, 1959, associated modern society and its media with 'psychic mobility', that is with a certain individual freedom to choose conceptual or cultural norms and definitions, an attitude characteristic of British Pop.

Up to 1960, there was very little pop-based fine art to be seen in public. When the second wave of Pop art appeared, it was accordingly not based on or reactive to exhibited art, even though many art students were familiar with reproductions of Johns and Rauschenberg. Its breeding ground was again the Royal College. It would be difficult to say whether the student sub-culture there was very different from that in other schools of art, being, no doubt, equally concerned with drink, sex, pop music, William Blake, movies etc, but the recurrence there of connected ideas, not specifically inculcated by staff, over a period covering several generations of students, argues that it was strong. It was a post-graduate school, its select students more sure of themselves than others. They had to face the continued international dominance of Abstract Expressionism and its associated theory. The integrity of the surface of most American Pop art shows that the younger artists had to go along with part of the AE ethic, even while affronting abstraction itself. Traces of art as action can be seen in the work of several of the English painters including Hockney and Boshier, also the sense that the canvas is not a window onto the world but a field of activity of the artist in which they could make any choice that interested them. Such choices might be expressed in any language in the continuum from high to low art, and from the media of writing, collage and representation to formal or informal abstraction. It was commonly understood that the style or language of the imagery was as much a carrier of information, assertion or persuasion as the iconography (implying, as it did, the cultural matrix of which it was a manifestation), and could be chosen as freely. The modernism of the work was defined by this fact, as well as by the assumption of the young that what concerns them is necessarily modern and, very often, by their reference to current personalities, images, topics and events. This choice was itself a constituent of their own style or styles. The artists described in the following paragraphs were liberated by the changes in awareness that had been proceeding in the late 50s and could create their work with little deliberation and theory.

The first and decisive manifestation of the art that was to be called 'Pop' was at the student show, 'Young Contemporaries', February 1961. The students' committee of eight members included several who were to become known as Pop artists: Peter Phillips, President, Allen Jones, Secretary, and Derek Boshier. Among others selected were David Hockney, Patrick Caulfield, Ron Kitaj, as well as some who have been more distantly associated with Pop: Patrick Proctor (on the committee), Anthony Donaldson, David Oxtoby, Frank Bowling, Norman Toynton etc . . . The professional selection committee (appointed by the students) was divided between protagonists of various kinds of abstract and representational art but among them was the critic Lawrence Alloway. He was asked to write the introduction, which distinguishes the nascent Pop from a realist group in whose work 'the subject is usually glimpsed through a massive screen of style,' and who 'seem to be struggle painters before they are realists'. Describing this group, he notes the concern with the city, graffiti and the imagery of mass communications. He does not identify the work as 'Pop art', a term he had coined to distinguish that imagery from both folk art and fine art, but writes, 'The impact of popular art is present, but checked by puzzles and paradoxes about the play of signs at different levels of signification. . .' Writing at the end of 1962,[7] Alloway is still doubtful about this art, which he finds incoherent, 'awkward arrays of different kinds of signs', lacking in a grasp of history and rather childish: 'Instead of contributing to the expanded communications system, which is 19th- and 20th-century art, they are coasting along and relaxing. Pop art in England has become a game for those who want to tell themselves that they 'think young'.

But perhaps Alloway had been thinking about all of this too long. Having invented the term 'Pop art', contributed to the culture out of which Pop art was to grow, and discerned many of the new art's characteristics quite accurately, he did not see its significance. He notes in the same introduction that 'the act of sending in to the Young Contemporaries . . . shows an ambition to be an artist which is far from universal in art schools.' He might have added that, in choosing him, the foremost protagonist of an art of high international ambition (he was about to follow his own advice and move to New York where the most ambitious action was), the students were bidding for a place in that world. The instant success of their tactics was demonstrated in the amount of press coverage, in the immediate inclusion of several of the young artists in the John Moores Prize exhibition and other shows, and the take up of dealers. This may have been a game, but it was not child's play, as he implies.

Bradford R Collins has shown[8] how Warhol, the most radical as well as the most successful of American Pop artists, tested his styles to find the most effective and marketable. The function of Collins' essay was to bring Warhol up to date in terms of the success theory of artists of the 80s, like Jeff Koons. The gentlemanly casualness of most of the business of English dealers and critics in the early 60s did not present such a criterion, neither was success as such so obtrusively a target of the artists. What the young artists could do was to produce an art for an audience that showed a new interest in a wide range of cultural manifestations, particularly those associated with their own generation. It offered scope for detailed iconographic analysis (decoding), of which Alloway and Banham were the known practitioners. Although the popular arts were a large element of their referential field they were by no means the whole of it; fine art, architecture, art history and the high culture were equally their concern. But the Pop references brought them attention that other students did not receive. No insincerity is implied in this. In fact the defining characteristic of Pop art in Britain at this time was rather that each artist painted what for him or her (very few women) was 'my world'. This world was sometimes described as a 'landscape', implying a view of one's own environment. 'Cityscape' or even 'mediascape' may have been more appropriate but a more accurate comparison was that of the 'tackboard', as featured in 'This is Tomorrow', where one can pin up interesting images or comments, work in progress and agenda. It is an exteriorisation of one's mental furniture where ideas may be represented in any form, whether autograph or appropriated. As Ken Russell's film *Pop Goes the Easel* (1962) demonstrated, chosen objects could represent life-style, a foretaste of what was to come.

The primary influence in formulating an art of this kind was the advice of Ron Kitaj, an immigrant American, an older and more experienced artist. Little of his material was derived from the popular arts, most from the stock and publications of the same intelligentsia that the ICA group had sought to transcend. In terms of their pictorial organisation, only a small number of his works, often prints, resemble tack boards, most of the others, though sharing the same diversity of reference and style, are tragedies expressed in terms of what he called 'plural energies'. They lament the decay of the culture of socialism as it becomes institutionalised. Although the emotional charge was high, the titles and the commentaries that he began to publish very soon multiplied the associational dimensions implied by the aggregated imagery. They presuppose that the works are up to a point readable by participants and anyone willing to learn.

OVERLEAF: The Pop Art Show, Royal Academy, London, (left to right) Eduardo Paolozzi, Solo, *1962; Peter Phillips,* Forces Sweetheart – Synchronised, *1962,* Purple Flag, *1960; Peter Blake,* Toy Shop, *1962,* Kim Novak Wall, *1959; RB Kitaj,* Good News for Incunabulists *(photo Stephen White)*

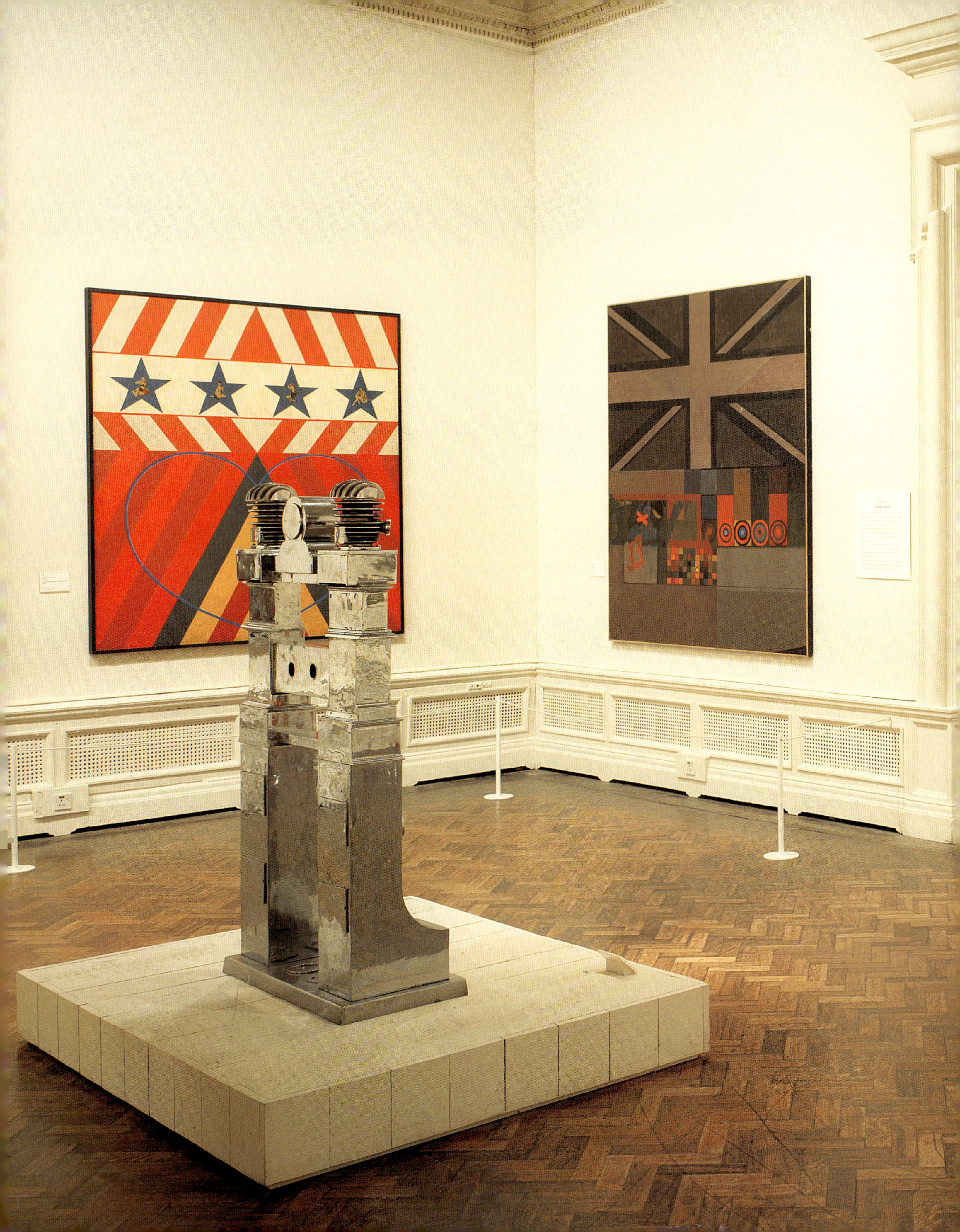

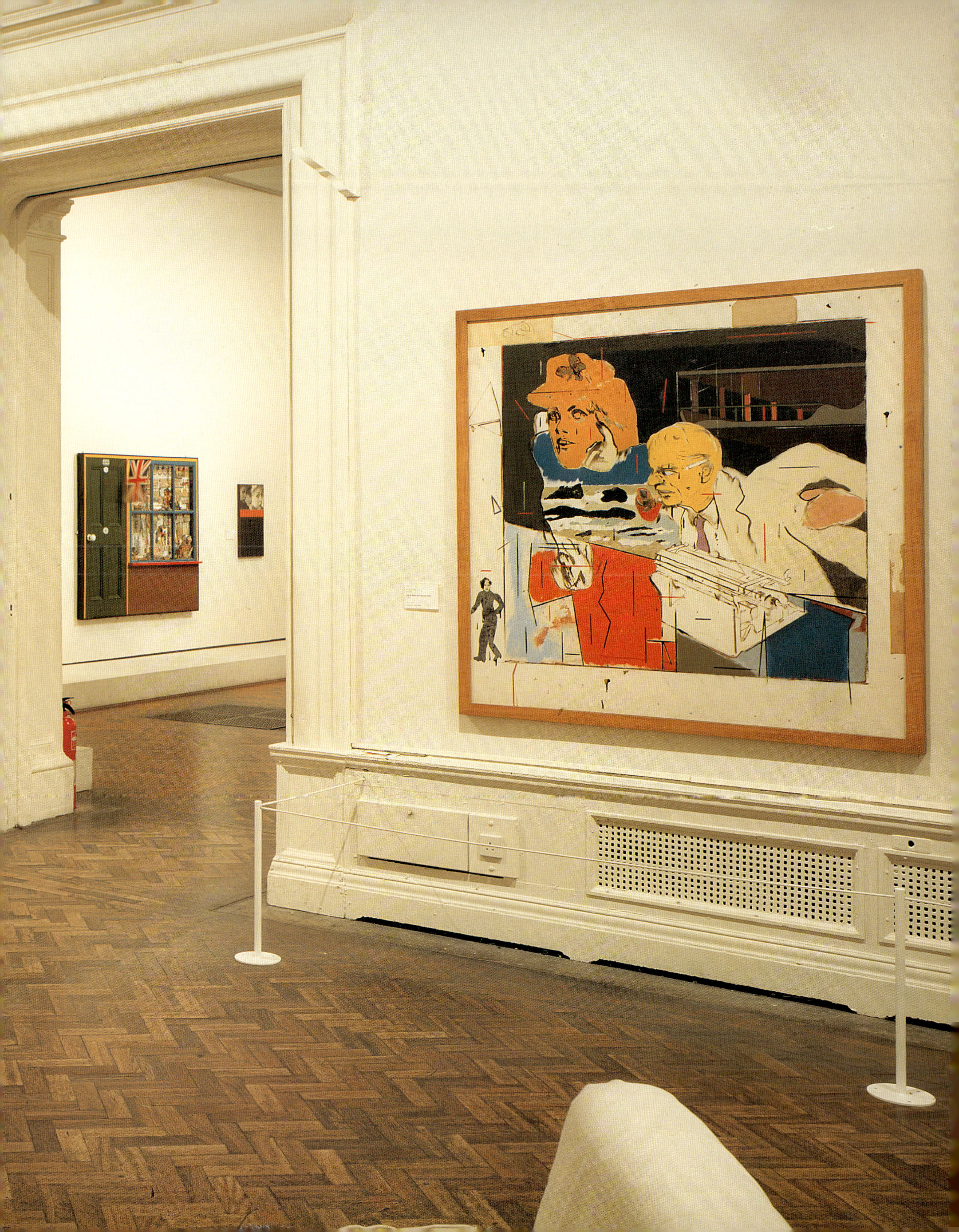

Kitaj helped the younger David Hockney by encouraging him to dedicate his painting to what concerned him most. In his early 20s, this consisted largely in his sexuality, morality and having a good time, all of which included exploiting his own virtuosity as a painter. That none of this was trivial or unradical is attested by the social history of the subsequent decades. Hockney revealed his homosexuality, at first thinly disguised in coded references and quotations, but, not long after, he was frankly to paint the objects of his fantasy and desire. The style he chose for the early works was itself referential: it suggested the disarming naivety of children's drawing and graffiti, but also, for those in the know, the sophistication of certain major contemporaries, Dubuffet and Bacon and, more distantly, Klee and Grosz, who had brought into fine art features of graphics that extended its powers of carrying meaning. In the early 60s, many of Hockney's paintings make play with variations of style, which, especially when associated with autobiographical references, may be considered a metaphor for the artist's refusal to be confined to a role conditioned or forced upon him or to see the world according to a single notion of reality. As Hockney himself has pointed out, his work has continued to oscillate between the interests of the medium and of the object, to which one may add desire or human need.

Derek Boshier's painting was more evidently concerned with contemporary events and used contemporary imagery. But his prevailing themes were commercial dehumanisation and the invasion of American culture, both very topical at the time. His style remained quite painterly, but his language of persuasion was graphic, emulating the devices of magazine advertising but turning it against itself. He was not afraid of banal metaphors: *England's Glory*, 1961, has not only the Stars and Stripes encroaching on the Union Jack, but a quotation of 'England expects. . .' and even the old school tie. The painting leaves open the question of what, in a culture whose glory is represented by a debased match-box cover image of a 19th-century gunboat, is worth defending against the American incursion. Does the transfer of the top of the match box to the bottom of the picture imply the suspended or illusory movement of a film? Ambiguity pervades the work; a knowledgeable and right-thinking audience, that is, one capable of making its own judgements, is implied. It is also self selected as that which will respond to a complex painting of this type. After a short time Boshier switched to a type of abstract Pop in which the message is encoded in style alone. Later he reverted to a more explicitly critical type of work.

American contemporaries, like Lichtenstein and Warhol, could eliminate most of the art references from their work and still rely on the highly developed market and critical culture to locate it as art. In England, the painters had to embody more conspicuous elements of the fine art tradition in their work so as to give point to what was new. Allen Jones' resources included motifs from high and low culture, ignoring any distinction between them, and so exemplifying the cultural continuum argued by Alloway. The structure of his first paintings was consciously modelled on an impeccable high art source, the early abstraction of Kandinsky. No doubt Jones was aware of the universalism of Kandinsky's notion of art expressed in the eclecticism of the Almanach, 'Der Blaue Reiter', but the openness of the earlier artist's composition and notations made them appropriate to the poetics of Jones' art. The metaphor of (almost complete) fusion of opposites recurs in Jones' work, high and low culture, male and female, person and object. Later, as Pop art in general and his own in particular established their own sub-culture, he could be as direct or as elusive as he liked, leaving the uncultured to complain of both.

Patrick Caulfield's rather later *Engagement Ring* seems as uncomplicated as some contemporary American art, but there were no specifically American references at this time and, although he devised techniques to banalise his imagery (whatever its source), his paintings in the 60s were principally concerned with pictorial considerations, especially the relationship of pattern to composition and to expression. This might involve apparent parody of American high art, for instance Judd's boxes as battlements.

Of the British artists most closely associated with Pop, only Peter Phillips made commercial imagery the dominant (but still not exclusive) theme of his work. Early pieces, like those of several of our artists, make use of the imagery of games, especially slot machines. This metaphor does not have a constant meaning; it could be associated with the logic of control, the tactics of choice or the alienation of motive. However the core of Phillips' work is a long series of paintings in which highly realised images from a number of sources, technical and promotional, are brought together so as to add meaning to one another. Usually, each fragment has its own distinct spatial convention so that, as in Kandinsky's later paintings, space is not constructed as a single view. Nevertheless the sharp focus and assertiveness of the images suggests the certainty of a culture that the artist finds perfectly natural to him and perhaps his generation.

In the early 60s a number of artists whose sensibility had been close to Pop brought in or re-emphasised Pop imagery in their work, among them Richard Smith, Peter Blake and Joe Tilson. All had been at the Royal College and were, to some extent, involved in the sub-culture from which Pop came. But the changes in their work at this time may have had as much to do with the intense public interest in pop music, fashion etc, and the social changes which these both expressed and helped to generate, as with the success of Pop art itself. In the case of Tilson, for example, this work is only one episode in a continuing programme of constructing art around references to rich systems of thought.

Beginning two or three years later than the painters, several sculptors made work that can loosely be considered Pop in that it quotes (or parodies) received images and popular styles. Among them, Nicholas Monro, Jann Haworth and Clive Barker made works which linger in the memory longer than many of the paintings. One reason for this is that each work, even if made of many parts, is integral in style and iconography. That is it is without the multiple, grafted references and sign systems of most of the British painting. It corresponds in this sense, though not in sensibility, to American Pop, by this time well known to young artists.

Pop art, partly because of the catchy name that was pinned to it, and partly because of its actual qualities, quickly achieved public awareness. Other artists and students joined in, but this phase lasted no more than about five years, 1961-66, a short time for Britain, where movements continue to recruit adherents for longer than elsewhere. Nevertheless all the artists mentioned have continued to develop consistently during three decades, and Pop played a part in generating later movements. One line of descent was the practice of appropriating and recycling imagery common to a number of British artists including Keith Milow. Many more artists ransacked the whole range of possibilities of making art of what pleased and interested them, rather than what was demanded by the march of Modernism. In a more oblique way, the Independent Group's interest in semantics, cybernetics and images as sub-cultural indicators, descended through the teaching programme at colleges like Ealing (Roy Ascott, Bernard Cohen and others) to become part of the context of Conceptual art.

The student revolutions of 1968-69 not only politicised young artists but greatly accelerated the inflow of late Marxist ideas, procedures and vocabulary which have dominated ever since. Some artists have used advertising material of the same sort as have Pop artists, but the character of the 'deconstruction' intended suggests that only an elite within the intelligentsia is in control of its own language, thought and appetites. This sample is by Victor Burgin: 'The questions "for whom?" and "what?" are therefore to be dialectically related. In the following articles I suggest that, in the West, such a dialectic dictates that we first examine those codes and practices we know *de facto* to be mass consumed. It is these codes which enshrine the dominating ideology and it is therefore these codes which are to be deconstructed: hence the interest in advertising and photography. . .'[9] He shows some embarrassment that his art is not obviously 'for' the workers, but seems to elect himself to membership of 'the Cadres'. He made a number of works which resemble advertisements of a rather tasteful sort, which, with their captions, can be taken to deconstruct their commercial analogs. However, like much Pop art that may or may not be satirical, he leaves a degree of ambiguity. Only the deconstructors among the audience will see them as the artist does. Late Marxist deconstruction has been widely taught in art colleges and is practised in journals, so that an audience can be assumed. The trained response is what distinguishes some of the work of certain sculptors like Bill Woodrow and Julian Opie from Pop art, which it so strongly resembles. Other art uses images and words in a way related to Pop but in order to identify the artist with a political viewpoint, like that of Conrad Atkinson.

The closest inheritors of the position taken by Burgin (with other European artists) are mostly American. The generation of the late 80s includes both appropriators of images like Kruger and abstract artists like Halley, who show the same resistance to the demands of originality as the heroes of Pop to the extent that some works would not have looked out of place in the early 60s. The technique of success is just as evident, although it may be necessary to aim at several distinct audiences at the same time. Nevertheless, it is not much more than the accompanying text that distinguishes the aim. Some of the works of art are pleasant or amusing, others brash or garish. But the texts express an even greater and more pessimistic antagonism and become ever more obscure because behind every illusion is a simulacrum, after every demystification another deconstruction. Nobody claims to speak for the workers, but everyone is against the capitalists, the only resort is being an outsider, or 'utilising that process of corruption [of truth] as a poetic form'.[10]

In 1954 the American literary critic, Leslie Fiedler wrote, 'The self distrust of the [European] intellectuals, their loss of faith in their function and the value of their survival blends with the Marxist dogma that one's own bourgeoisie. . . is the worst enemy,' and shows that this bourgeoisie has been identified with America. '. . . American mass culture among the people moves inexorably into Europe. . . under our system you will survive. You will be harassed by movies, television, the comic books: but you will be permitted to fight back and you may win in the end.'[11] Europe has defended itself and won some engagements. Pop art itself helped to give artists, the public and even the intellectuals a means, a confidence and a freedom to do this. It was more than a straw in the wind of cultural pluralism.

NOTES

1 'Pop art' or 'Pop' is used here to mean a kind of fine art as distinct from 'pop' or 'popular' art, which means the kinds of mass-produced imagery often quoted in the former. See Lawrence Alloway, 'Pop Art: The Words', *Auction*, February 1968, pp6-9.

2 The word 'sub-culture', often used in the 50s, did not mean an inferior or oppressed culture, but merely one which, being more or less distinctive itself, was part of a larger complex or national culture; an individual normally belongs to several such sub-cultures.

3 Roland Barthes, 'The New Citroën', 1956, anthologised in *Mythologies,* 1957.

4 Published in Richard Hamilton, *Collected Words*, 1982, pp135-146. This lecture and that cited below were on design not fine art.

5 *ibid*, pp150-156.

6 Dwight MacDonald (ex-Trotskyite author of *A Theory of Mass Culture*, 1953) in *Encounter*, November 1956, p17.

7 Lawrence Alloway, '"Pop Art" since 1949', *The Listener*, 27 December 1962.

8 Bradford R Collins, 'The Metaphysical Nosejob: the Remaking of Warhola, 1960-1968', *Arts Magazine*, February 1988, pp47-55.

9 Victor Burgin, *Two Essays on Art Photography and Semiotics*, 1976, p2. He is now teaching in California.

10 Ashley Bickerton in 'From Criticism to Complicity', *Flash Art,* no 129, May 1986, p46.

11 'The Good American' in *Encounter*, II no 3, March 1954, pp51-53. The article follows one by Reyner Banham and so is likely to have been seen by IG members. JB Priestley replied to Fiedler in the expected fashion: ... Some of us would argue that once mass communications are raised to a certain level of power and efficiency . . . people can be manipulated to want what is convenient to give them . . . the American mind with its great talent for satire, provides most of the best antidotes for its own poisons.' This was the attitude confronted by Hamilton (notes 4 and 5), Banham and Alloway etc.

Patrick Caulfield, Stained Glass Window, *1967, oil, 213.4x121.9cm*

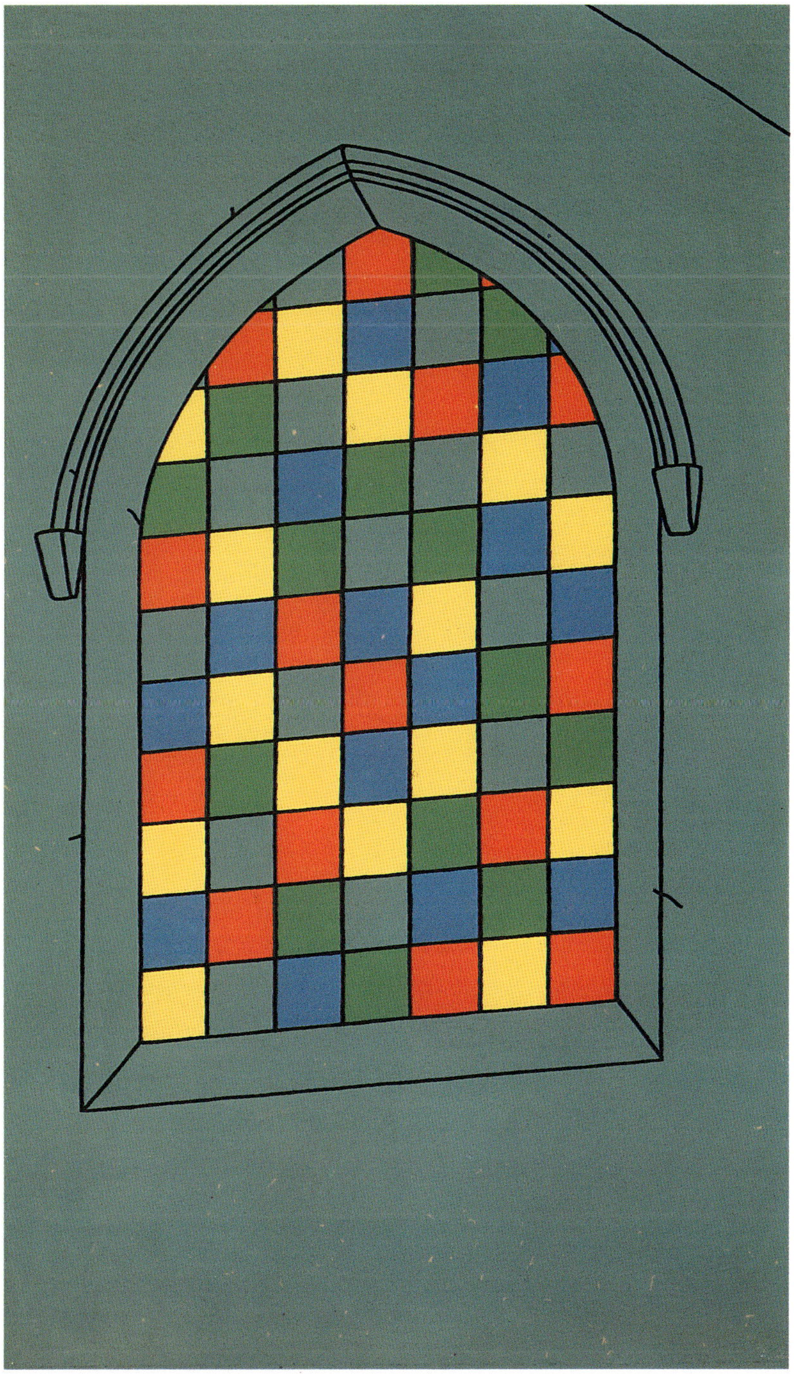

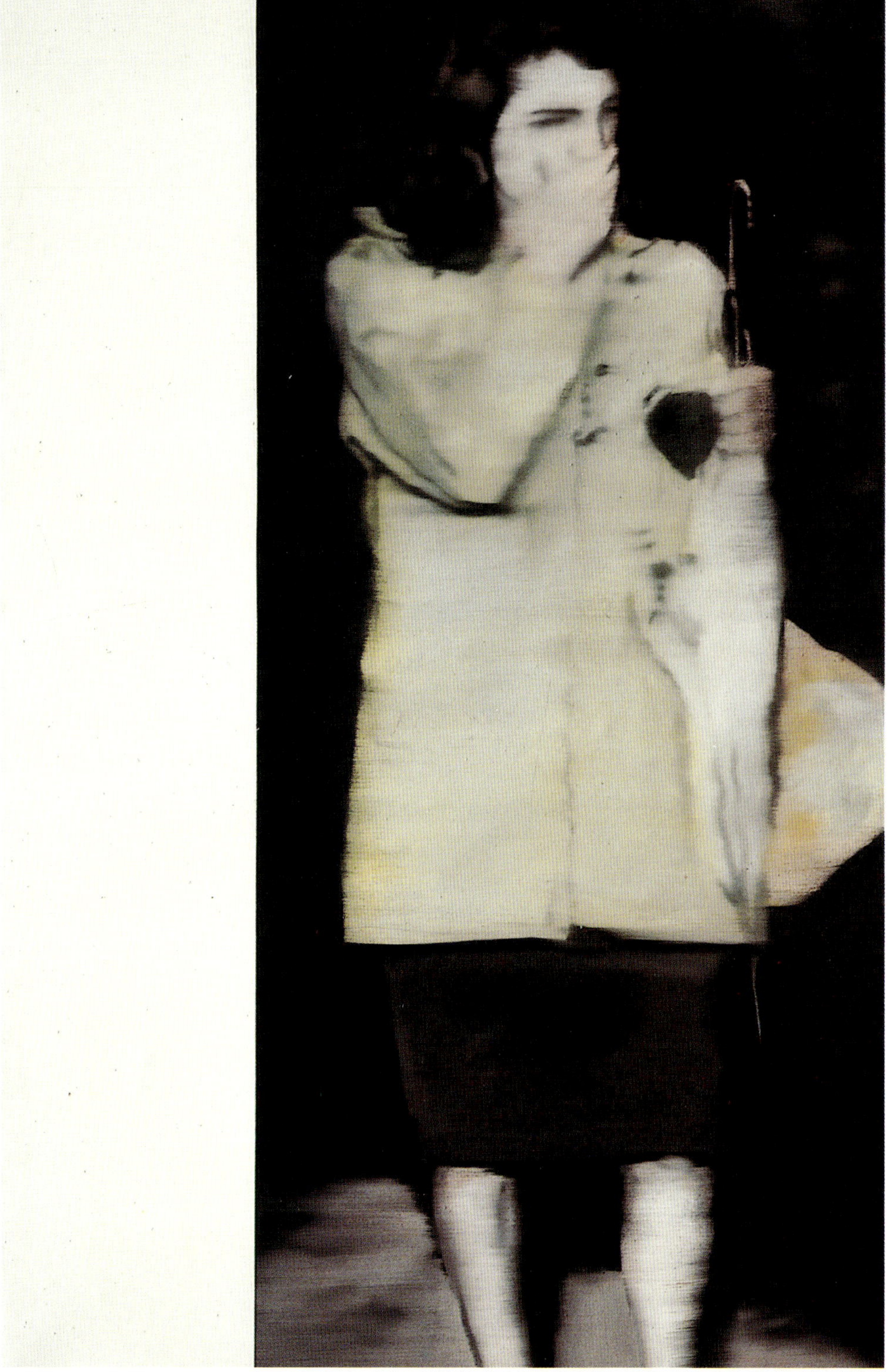

MARCO LIVINGSTONE

MODERNE KUNST: EUROPEAN POP, 1960s AND AFTER

The following extracts are taken from Marco Livingstone's new book Pop Art: A Continuing History *published by Thames and Hudson, London, 1990:*

Pop never developed as a coherent movement on the European Continent, although a number of artists separately contributed significantly to the expansion of its terms during the 1960s. Chief among these was Martial Raysse, who by 1962 had moved beyond his Nouveau Réaliste assemblages of found objects towards a more specifically pictorial style in which such objects were subservient to flat, mechanically derived images in bright artificial colours. In September 1962 Raysse was invited to take part in an exhibition at the Stedelijk Museum in Amsterdam, 'Dylaby (Dynamisch Labyrint)', which made explicit the concept of the room-sized installation as a participatory setting that had been explored during the previous few years by Americans such as Dine and Oldenburg and in British exhibitions such as 'This is Tomorrow' (1956) and 'Place' (1959). For this occasion Raysse recreated the carefree holiday atmosphere of his native French Riviera in an elaborate environmental work titled *Raysse Beach,* which was reassembled in November as his first one-man show in New York. In it he made use of numerous forms of representation that were drawn equally from the processed images of the mass media and from the merchandise of mass production: life-size photographic images of women, enlarged from the pages of fashion magazines and tinted in bright colours, were placed among real objects (including beach toys, a plastic swimming pool and a juke-box), in a setting conspicuously labelled with a neon sign. [. . .]

Unlike Warhol, who exploited the indefinite reproducibility of the image as a way of commenting on the numbing repetitiveness of modern life, Raysse used such methods largely to suggest a disembodied quality for motifs that were destined to remain unattainable mirages. Like other European Pop artists and in distinction from most American Pop, Raysse involved himself with narrative and expressed an emotional commitment to his subject-matter. [. . .]

Another French painter who developed his own form of Pop in the early 1960s was Alain Jacquet, initially in a series of paintings based on the decorative format of board games. [. . .] Although Jacquet liked the work of the Nouveaux Réalistes he never became close to the group, not only because most of them were about ten years or more older than he but because he preferred to work within the terms of modernist painting. He immediately felt close, however, to Raysse, who was similar in age and who by this time was working more as a painter than as a sculptor. They became friends and the two most important representatives in France of an idiom that could accurately be described as Pop. Yet it was only in 1963, when British and American Pop began to be shown in Paris, that Jacquet came across other art with which he felt sympathetic.

Jacquet was self-taught as a painter, but he had studied architecture briefly in 1960 at the Ecole des Beaux-Arts in Paris and as a Frenchman was aware of new trends such as semiology earlier than most of his counterparts in English-speaking countries; many of the early critiques published about his work

Gerhard Richter, Woman with Umbrella, *1964, oil on canvas 160x95cm. This work formed part of the Gerhard Richter exhibition at the Tate Gallery, London, 30 October 1991-12 January 1992. 'With this painting, I gave it a large margin: Warhol's paintings treated the image in a way that you could imagine the image continuing indefinitely either side of the canvas. With my picture the large printed margin separates the image within the painting from surrounding reality. I gave it a deliberately anonymous, neutral title, because I did not want people simply to look at it and instantly recognise Jackie Kennedy. I was very apprehensive about that sort of reaction. With a title like* Woman with Umbrella, *it doesn't reveal anything or tell any particular story . . . I was very moved by her fate expressed through gesture.' (Interview with Sean Rainbird, 1991)*

OVERLEAF: The Pop Art Show, Royal Academy, London, (left to right) Alain Jacquet, Birth of Venus, *1963;* Déjeuner sur l'Herbe, *1964-65; Martial Raysse,* Rose, *1962,* Simple and Quiet Painting, *1965 (photo Stephen White)*

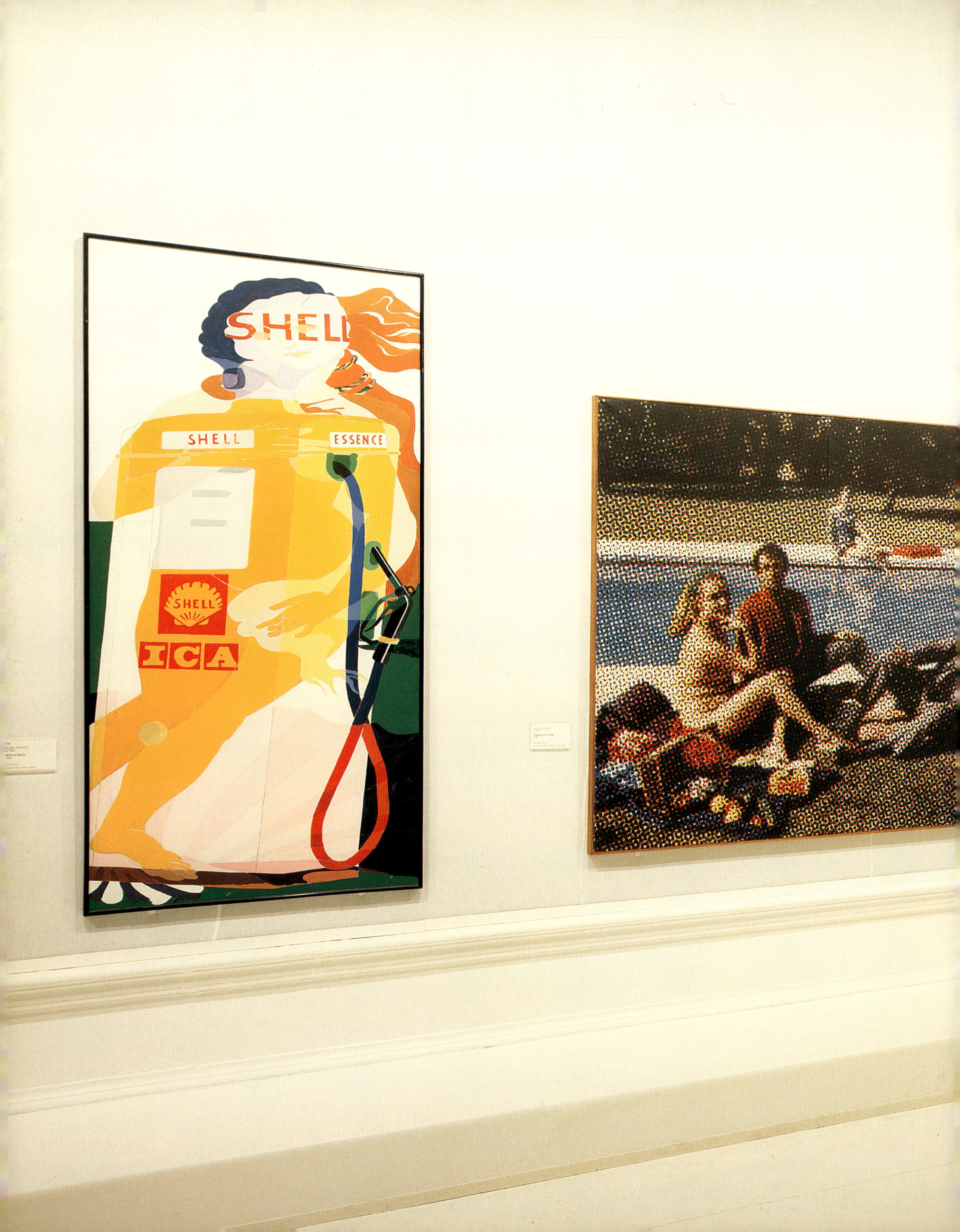
SHELL
SHELL
ESSENCE
SHELL
ICA

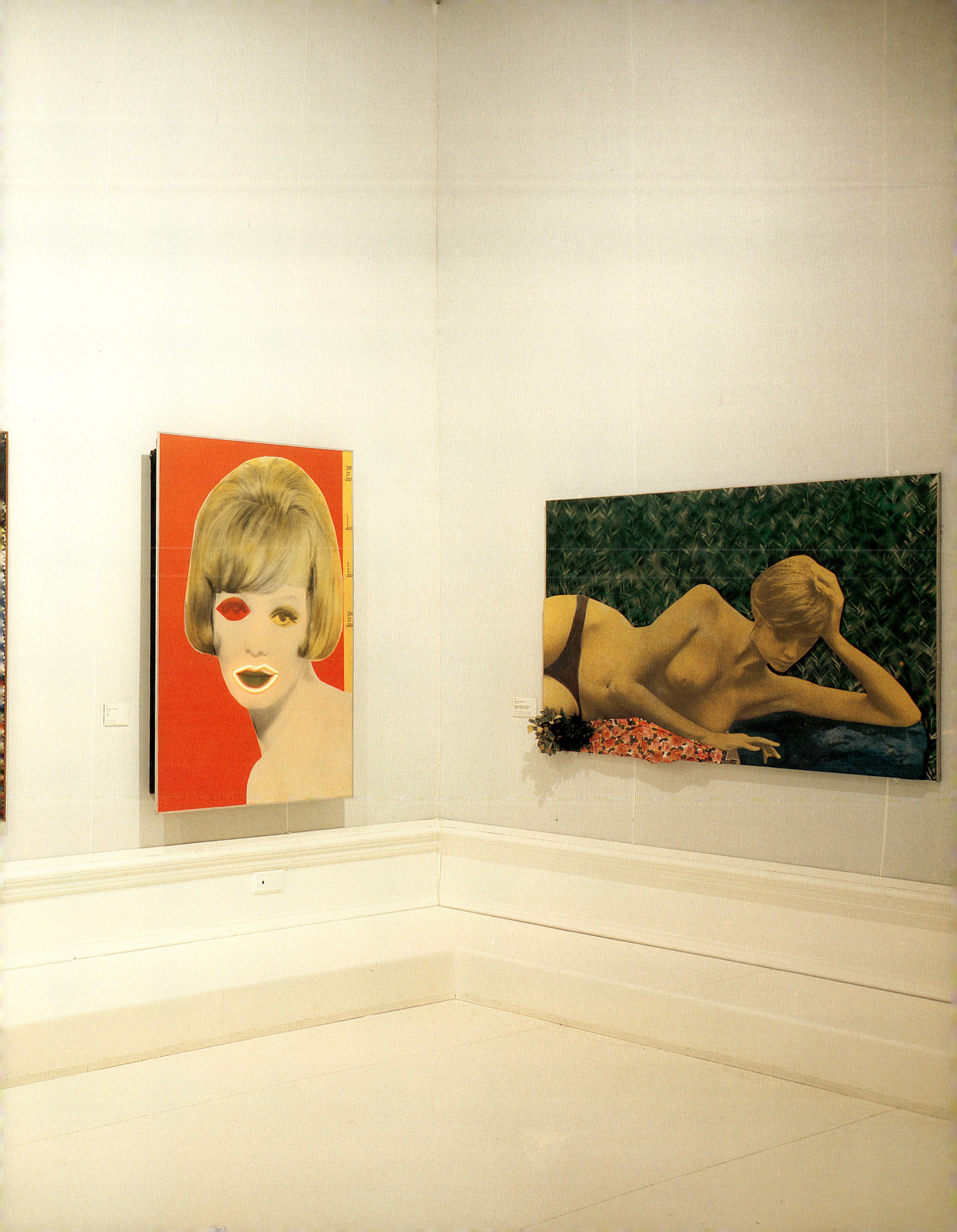

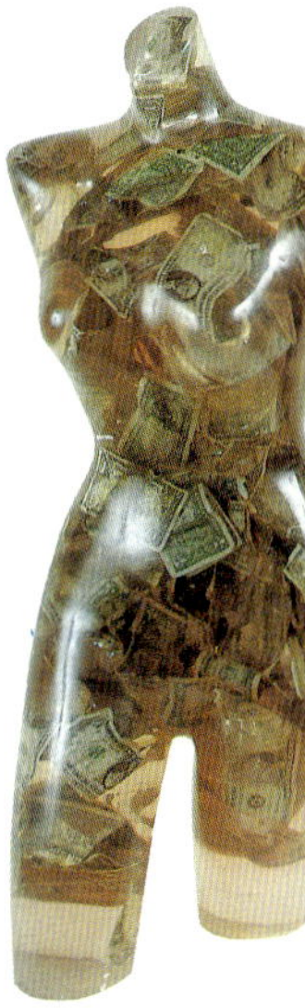

Arman, Vénu$, Poupée dollars*, 1970, dollar bills embedded in polyester mannequin form, 92x31x27cm*

in France set it into the context of this philosophical method of analysis. Although it was more a question of being involved with similar ideas than with a desire to illustrate them, the works he produced during the first half of the 1960s were consequently as highly conceptual as those produced anywhere during that period. In 1962 he began a series of paintings entitled *Camouflages*: each is of a hand-painted rendering of a reproduction of a famous work partly obscured by a blatantly contemporary image or crude abstract pattern. [. . .]

A central concern of Jacquet's early work was the gradual dissolution of a motif that could still be read because of our previous knowledge, and it is for this reason – rather than for an essentially parodic intent – that so many of his pictures of the early to mid-1960s were based on familiar images from the history of art. The increasing complexity of the stages by which he removed a particular motif from its original context was indicated by his anamorphic treatment of a painting-by-number rendition of Leonardo's *Last Supper*. In 1964 he painted an extended series of variations of Manet's *Déjeuner sur l'herbe* of 1865, in which he introduced a new way of working that extended the ideas he had been exploring during the previous two or three years. [. . .]

Although in 1965 Restany devised the term Mec Art (from Mechanical Art) to describe works by Jacquet and other artists (including Rotella, the Belgian Pol Bury and the Greek Nikos) based on the appropriation of photographic images, Jacquet maintains that while he was happy to use mechanical procedures he was not obsessed by them. He liked the simplicity of the process but was prepared to use other methods to achieve a similar fragmentation of an image derived from photography. [. . .] The intertwined themes of Jacquet's Pop works – that of the ambiguity of vision and of the dialogue between what is 'fake' and what is 'authentic' – gradually took him into more purely conceptual areas and away from Pop imagery. [. . .]

As early as 1962, in works such as *Marilyn Monroe* (Marilyn Idolo), Vostell had begun to manipulate the found images used in his *décollages* by partly obliterating them in smears of paint in the manner of Rauschenberg. By 1965 he was using photographs, silk-screened photographic images and real objects as a means of juxtaposing and layering found images in works such as *Car Crash* (1965-7), where the horrific nature of the subject-matter is held in abeyance by its co-existence with the sweet colouring, abstract textures and decorative pattern that first attract one's eyes to the surface. In other works of this period, such as *Wir waren so eine Art Museumsstück* (We were a Kind of Museum Piece, 1964), he likewise combined mechanical or semi-mechanical techniques with a variety of media images, here a newspaper headline, photographs of street fighting and a repeated image of Lee Harvey Oswald being assassinated. [. . .]

Like Vostell, Richter and Lueg each relied on blatantly photographic images, although they replicated them in paint in wholly different ways: Richter, as a painter of extraordinary facility, used conventional brushes to approximate the surface of slightly out-of-focus black-and-white photographs, while Lueg exaggerated tonal contrasts to achieve a poster-like immediacy of image. In the mid-1960s Polke, who like Richter and Lueg was student at the Staatliche Kunstakademie in Düsseldorf, also devised a quasi-mechanical system for replicating colour photographs in his oil paintings, using superimposed patterns of dots reminiscent of half-tone printing. In 1963 they invented the term Capitalist Realism to describe their ironic embrace of materialism; it was a deliberate echo of the official Socialist Realism of the Communist states, as both Polke and Richter were from East Germany. It was only in the most general ways, however, that the work of these three artists could be taken as part of a common assault on the conventions of representational painting. All three were regarded in the early literature of Pop as minor followers of the movement, if they were mentioned at all, but Richter and Polke emerged in the 1970s as among the most important post-war painters in Germany. [. . .]

In some of his earliest photographically derived paintings, such as *Terese Andeszka* (1964), Richter dutifully copied not only the found image but also the accompanying fragments of text – in this case, one presumes, part of its caption in a magazine – as a way of acknowledging that the motif has been lifted entirely from a printed source [. . .] By and large, however, Richter did not base his paintings on photographs already familiar to a wide public, as was the case with Warhol's film-star portraits or grisly disasters. Instead he favoured more ordinary private snapshots, at once intimate in their origins and anonymous. [. . .]

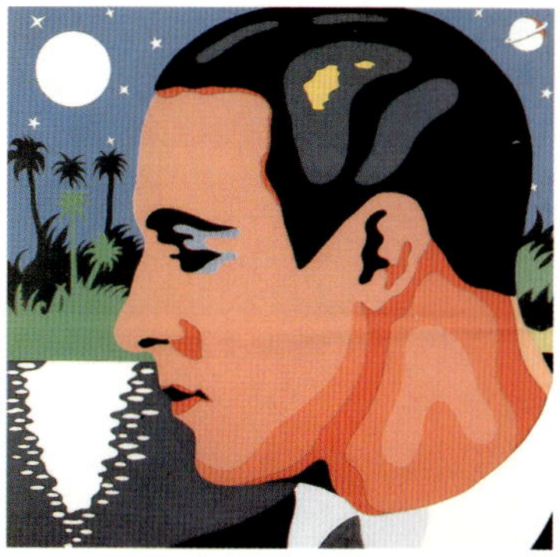

Equipo Crónica, Latin Lover*, 1966, acrylic, 120x120cm*

While evading the constrictions of a single style, Richter maintained an elegance of conception and delicacy of touch at all times. By contrast, Polke declared his freedom from a traditional conception of fine art by addressing himself to the most undignified pictorial conventions he could find and by mimicking them with a crudeness and brutality that was extreme even by the standards of American Pop. More than a decade passed before early paintings by him such as *Plastik-Wannen* (Plastic Tubs, 1964) and *Liebespaar II* (Couple II, 1965) could be appreciated as anything more than badly painted and misguided responses to Pop. Both these works have a deliberately rough and unfinished look that seems even more alarming because of the apparent effort that has gone into composing their obviously unworthy elements into a pleasing decoration. [. . .]

An idea intrinsic to much Pop has been that of a collaboration between low and high culture; Polke has simply taken this to an extreme by subjecting his artistic identity so completely to the conventions of bad painting that it is possible to forget that he remains in control and that such astonishing coarseness has been deliberately pursued in order to taunt us. [. . .]

From 1963 to 1969 Polke worked intermittently on a series of paintings based on the pseudo-mechanical replication of photographs: the generic term he used was *Rasterbild* (screen-picture) because of the way in which the image is reconstructed by a grid of coloured dots suggesting a grossly magnified half-tone reproduction. [. . .]

Another type of picture with which Polke concerned himself from 1964 to 1971, the *Stoffbild* (fabric picture), also constituted a reaction to Pop strategies with found material. Each of these pictures, such as *Palmen* (Palms, 1964), was painted on a piece of cloth chosen for its decorative pattern and used as a stereotypical 'modern art' background against which to place an equally trite pattern or image. While thus extending the notion of the painting as a real object established by Johns and other Pop artists, Polke shifted attention to the element of parody so as to challenge the belief in invention and authenticity that still prevailed among the avant-garde. These and other 1960s works by Polke, such as the slapdash travesty of gestural abstraction prominently and disrespectfully labelled *Moderne Kunst* (Modern Art, 1968), declared in no uncertain terms his belief that an artist could best become free of the limitations of style by making knowing reference to every pictorial convention available without seeming to subscribe to any with sincerity. [. . .]

Similar tactics were employed by other European artists during the 1960s, such as the Spanish group Equipo Crónica. This partnership, consisting of the painters Rafael Solbes and Manuel Valdés, was formed in Valencia in 1964 after an exhibition of contemporary Spanish art in which they had both taken part; they continued to work together until Solbes died in 1981. The very idea of working collaboratively, with the personality of each artist subjugated to the identity of their jointly produced work, was evidence of their predisposition to the tenets of Pop. [. . .]

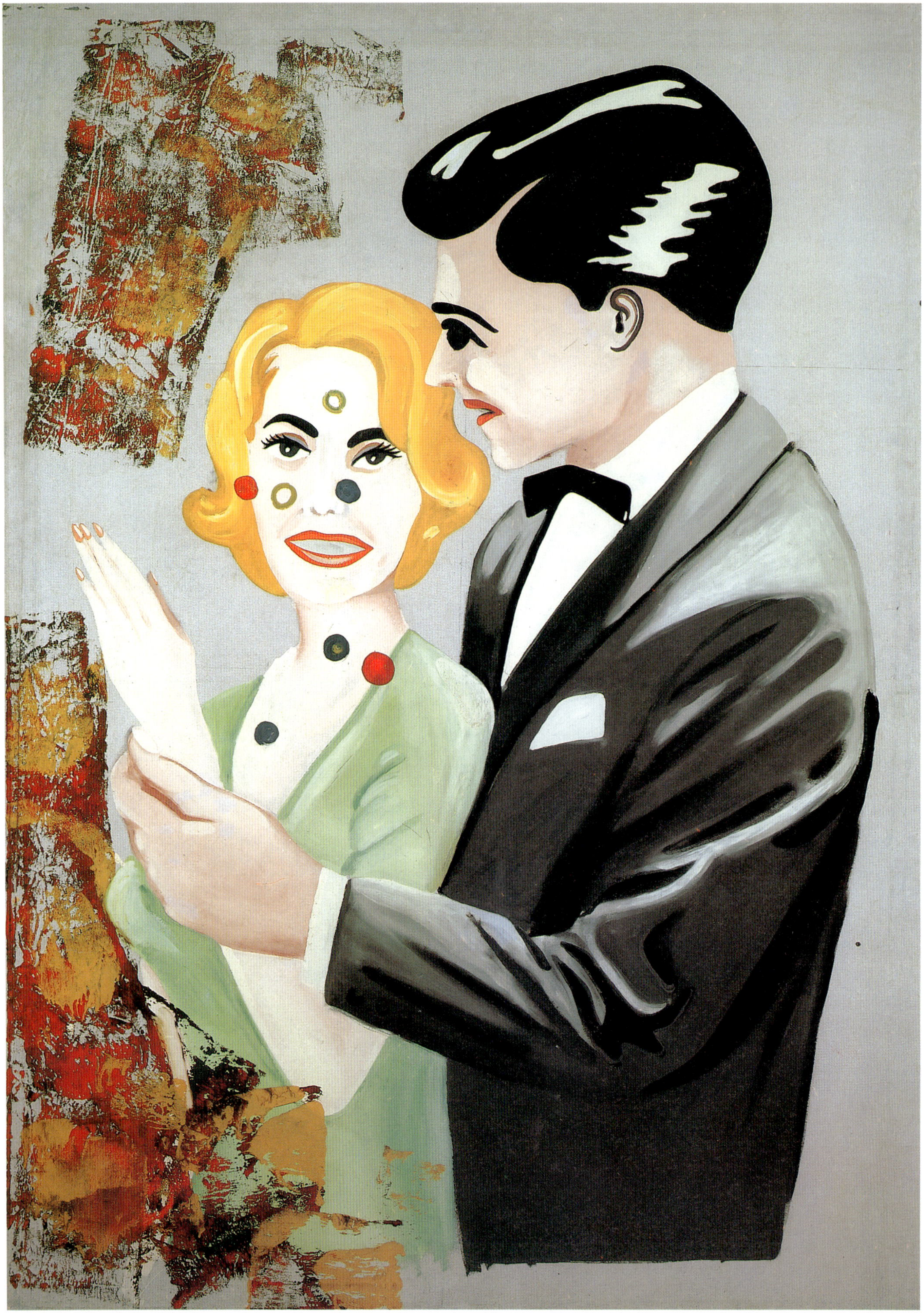

The progress of Pop ideas in later Continental art, as in its American and British counterparts, continued to return to the common object and to the question of reproduction. Arman, who of all the Nouveaux Réalistes remained most faithful to the system of recycling mass-produced objects that had characterised the first incursions of Continental artists into Pop territory, remained particularly well placed to elaborate such themes. After settling in New York in 1963, he tended for his 'accumulations' to favour newly purchased objects rather than used ones, as had often been the case in his Paris work. In *Vénu$, Poupée dollars* (Venu$, Dollar Doll, 1970) he also began to use moulded containers in transparent polyester, rather than simple box-like shapes, to establish a relationship between the outer image – here identified literally with human skin – and the internal contents. This equation between feminine beauty and commercial exploitation formed part of a series in which a youthful female torso was given a specific and often sexually charged identity. In *Venus of the Shaving Brushes* (1969), for instance, sexual union is suggested through the alliance of feminine smoothness and masculine beards, while in *Cold Petting* (1967) the body is filled with mannequin hands that appear to be groping her thighs and breasts from within, an even more disturbing image of penetration and invasion. The connotations of these images, although rooted to some extent in Surrealism, demonstrated unequivocally the continuing flexibility of purpose in Pop strategies. [. . .]

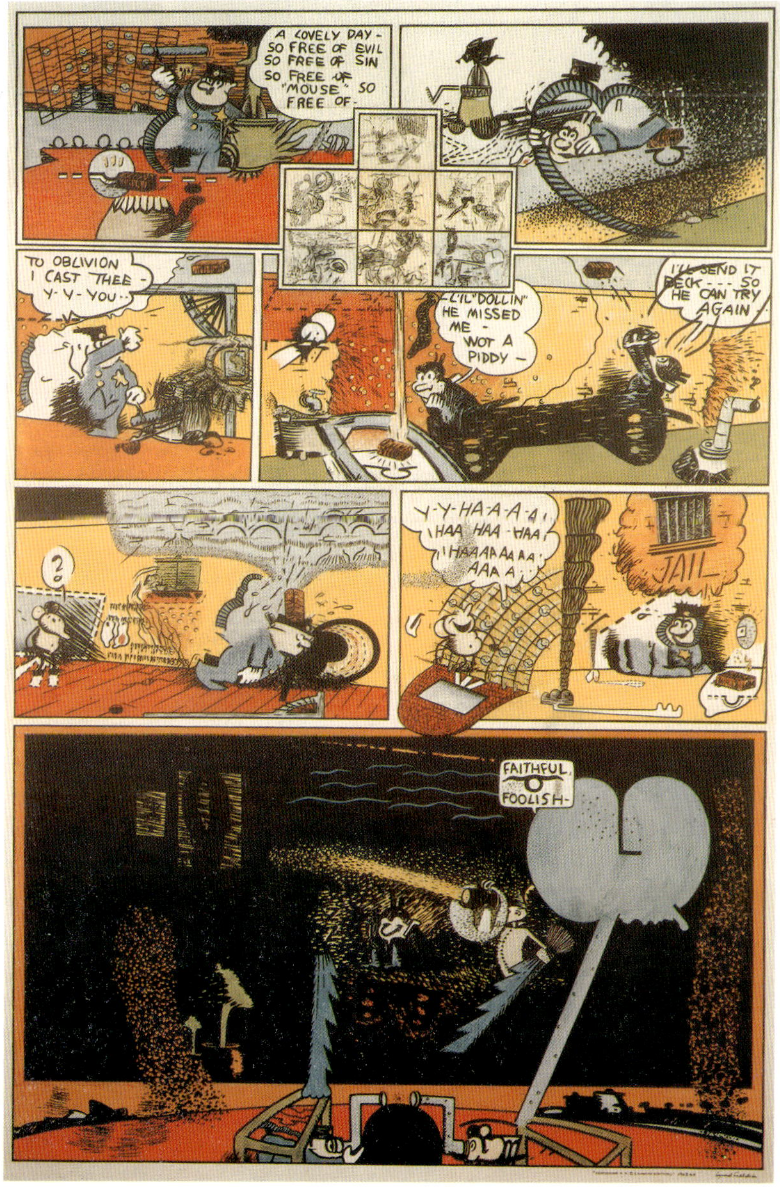

Sigmar Polke, Liebespaar II, *1965, oil and enamel, 190x150cm*

Oyvind Fahlström, Performing K K No 2 (Sunday Edition), *1963-64, tempera on paper, on canvas, 132x86.4cm. '. . . one of several works based on the character known as Krazy Kat, Fahlström appears interested not so much in the stylistic potential of such sources, or even in their identity as signs of contemporary culture, as in their narrative potential.'*

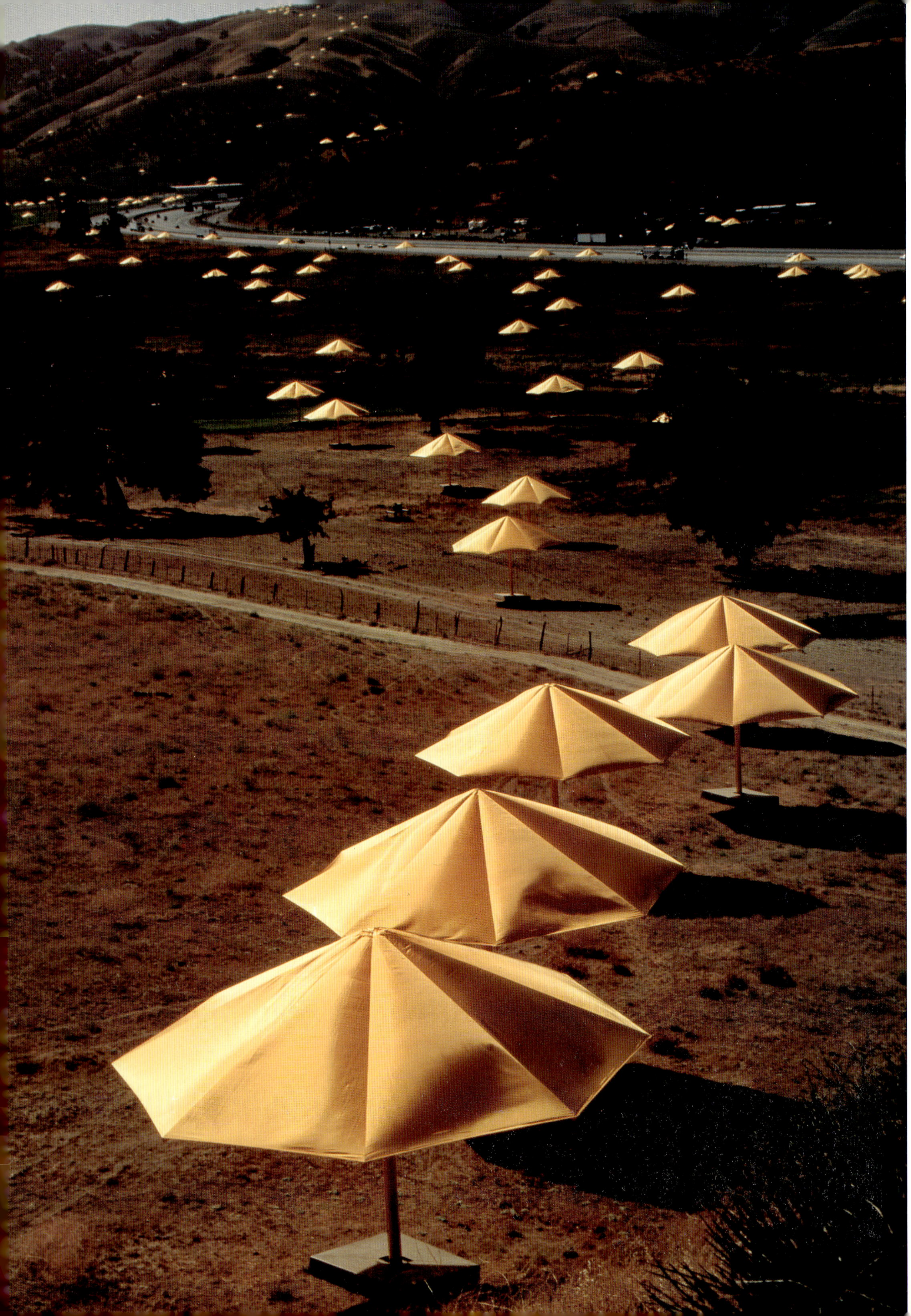

クリスト：アンブレラ 日本－アメリカ合衆国 1984－91
カリフォルニア、アメリカ側

CHRISTO: THE UMBRELLAS JAPAN – USA 1984-91
CALIFORNIA, USA SITE

CHRISTO

THE UMBRELLAS: JOINT PROJECT FOR JAPAN AND USA

At sunrise, on 9 October 1991, Christo's 1,880 workers began to open the 3,000 Umbrellas in Ibaraki and California. This Japan-USA temporary work of art reflects the similarities and differences in the ways of life and the uses of the land in two inland valleys, one 19km long in Japan, and the other 29km long in the USA. In Japan the valley is located north of Hitachiota and south of Satomi, 120 kms north of Tokyo, around Route 349 and the Sato River, in the Prefecture of Ibaraki, on the properties of 459 private landowners and governmental agencies. In the USA the valley is located 96km north of Los Angeles, along Interstate 5 and the Tejon Pass, between the south of Gorman and Grapevine, on the properties of Tejon Ranch, 25 private landowners as well as governmental agencies.

Eleven manufacturers in Japan, USA, Germany and Canada prepared the various elements of the Umbrellas: fabric, aluminium super-structure, steel frame bases, anchors, wooden base supports, bags and moulded base covers. Starting in December 1990, with a total work force of 500, Muto Construction Co Ltd in Ibaraki, and AL Huber & Son in California installed the earth anchors and steel bases. The sitting platform/base covers were placed during August and September 1991. From 19 September to 7 October 1991, an additional construction work force was engaged in transporting the Umbrellas to an upright closed position. On 4 October, students, agricultural workers, and friends, 960 in the USA and 920 in Japan, joined the work force to complete the installation of the Umbrellas.

Christo's $26m temporary work of art is entirely financed by the artist through The Umbrellas, Joint Project for Japan and USA Corporation of which Jeanne-Claude Christo-Javacheff is the president. Previous projects by the artist have all been financed in a similar manner through the sale of his studies, preparatory drawings, collages, scale models, early works and original lithographs. The artist does not accept any sponsorship.

The removal will start on 31 October and the land will be restored to its original condition. The Umbrellas will be taken apart and all elements will be recycled. The Umbrellas, free-standing dynamic modules, reflect the availability of the land in each valley, creating an invitational inner space, as houses without walls, or temporary settlements and relate to the ephemeral character of the work of art. In the precious and limited space of Japan, the Umbrellas are positioned intimately, close together and sometimes following the geometry of the rice fields. In the luxuriant vegetation enriched by water all the year round, the Umbrellas are blue. In the California vastness of uncultivated grazing land, the configuration of the Umbrellas is whimsical and spreading in every direction. The brown hills are covered by blond grass, and in that dry landscape, the Umbrellas are yellow. From 9 October, 1991 for a period of three weeks, *The Umbrellas* will be seen, approached, and enjoyed by the public, both by car from a distance and closer as they border the roads, or by walking under *The Umbrellas* in their luminous shadows.

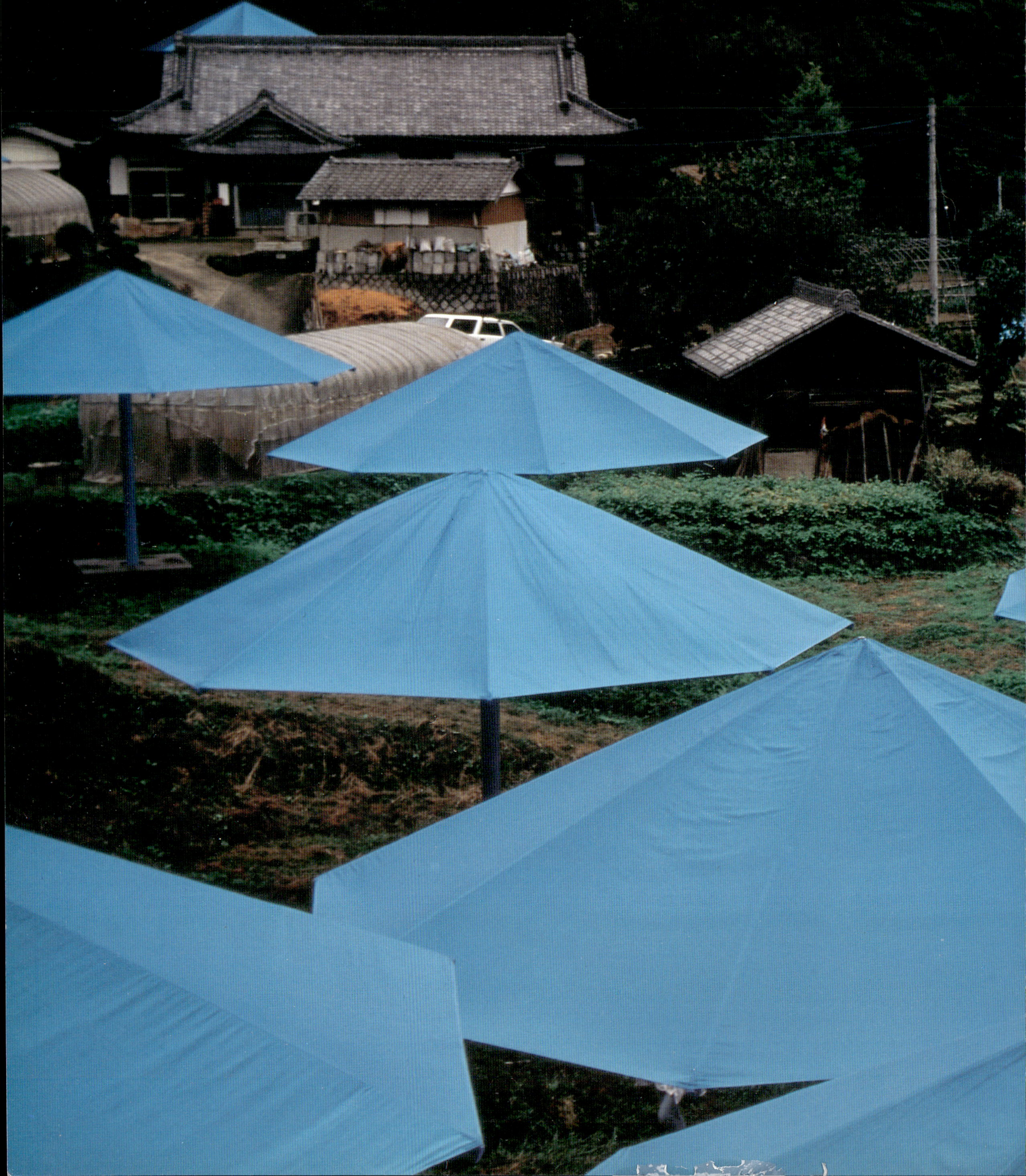

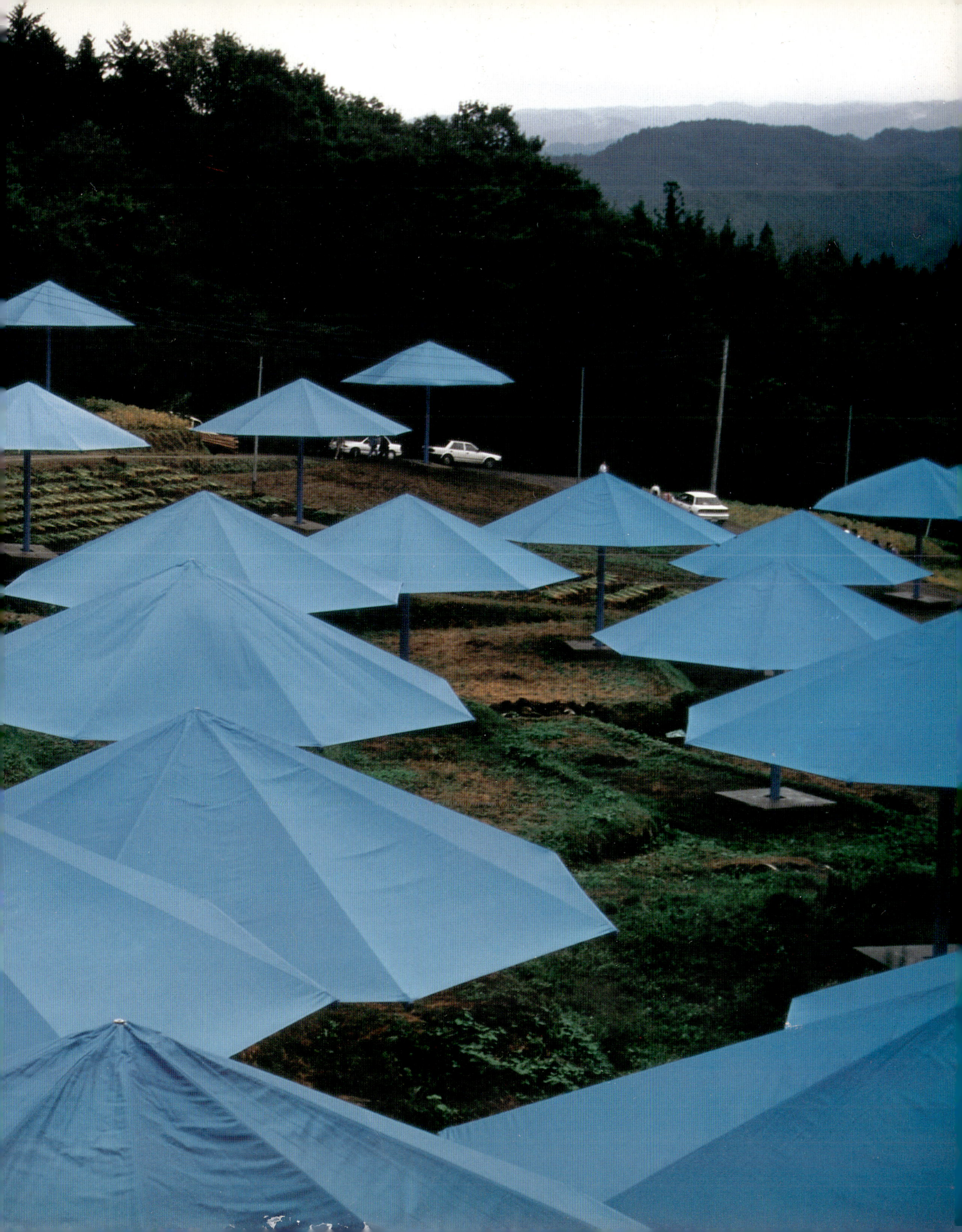

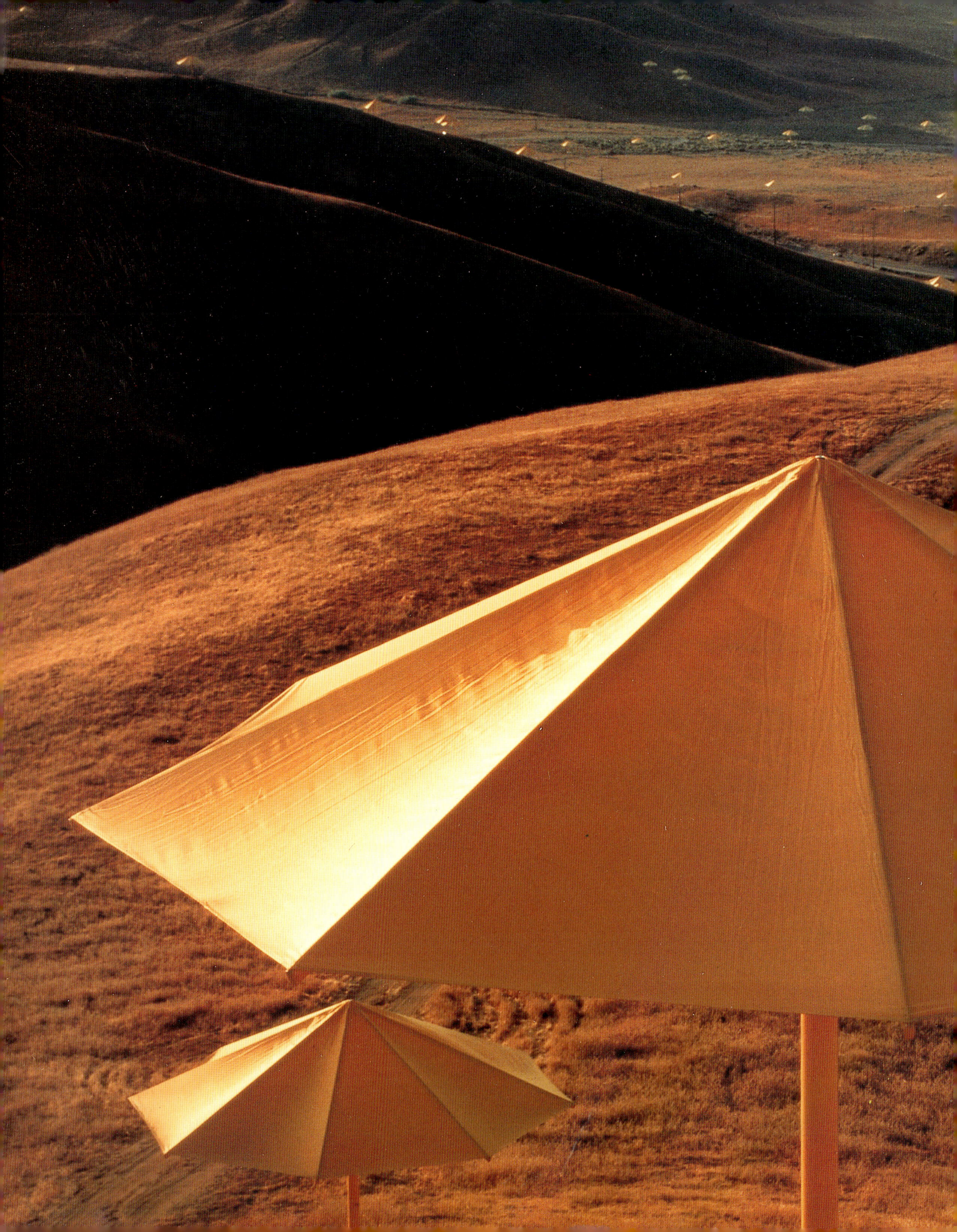

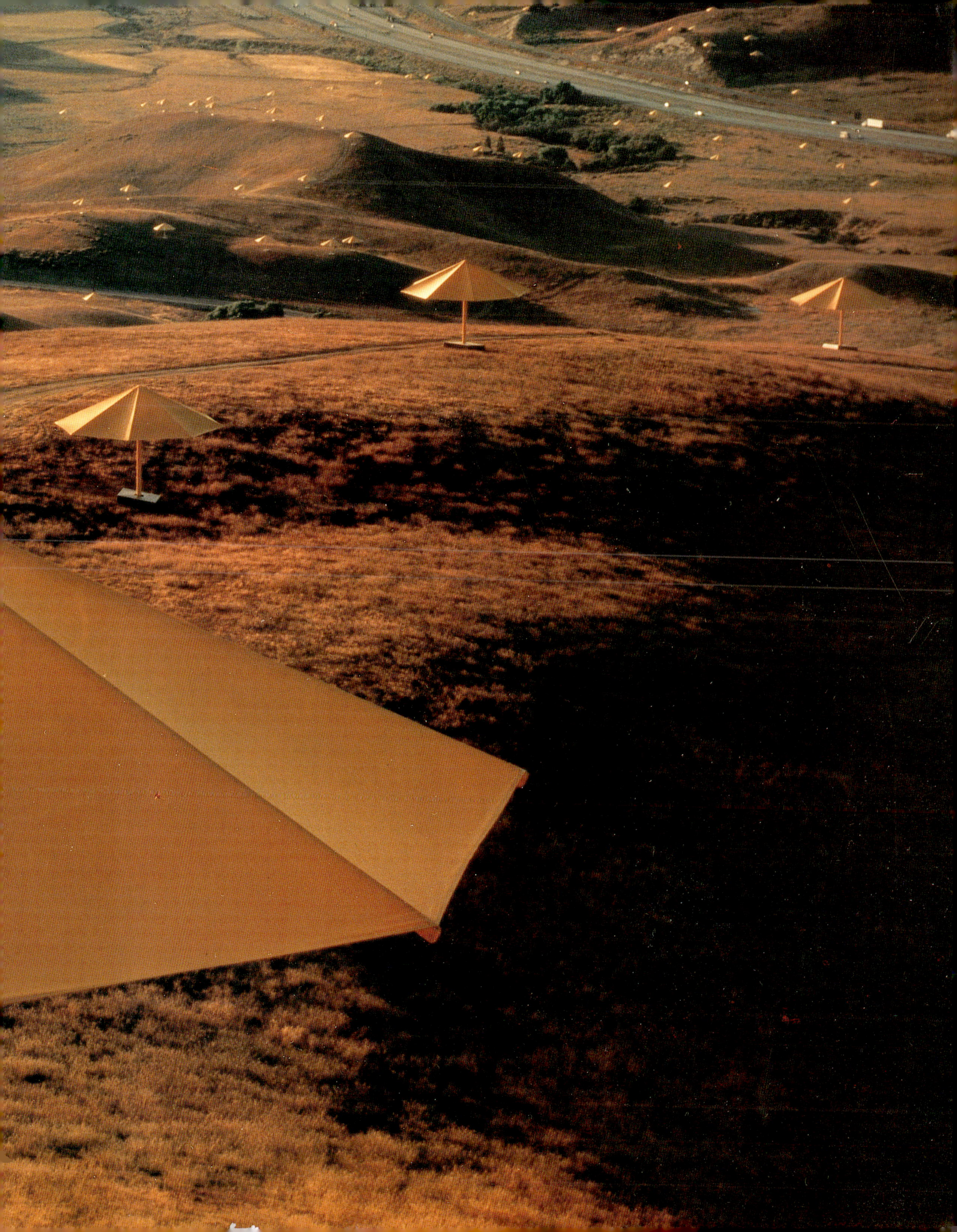

GOVERNMENTAL AGENCIES

TOKYO
Ministry of Construction
Building Centre
Ministry of Foreign Affairs

IBARAKI PREFECTURE
The Governor's Office
Planning Department
Public Works Department

HITACHIOTA-SHI
The Mayor's Office
Planning Division
Tokyo Electric Power, Hitachiota Office
Nippon Telegraph and Telephone, Hitachiota Office

HITACHI-SHI
The Mayor's Office
Planning Division
Hitachi Huto Co Ltd, Hitachi Port

SATOMI-MURA
The Mayor's Office
Planning Division

OMIYA-MACHI
River Kuji Fishermen's Union

WASHINGTON DC
US Department of the Interior, Bureau of Land Management
US Department of Transportation, Federal Aviation Administration
US House of Representatives
US Customs Service

STATE OF CALIFORNIA
The Governor's Office
Department of Transportation (Caltrans), District 6 and District 7
Department of Parks and Recreation
California Highway Patrol
Board of Equalisation
California Legislature, Assembly and Senate
Assembly Standing Committee on Revenue and Taxation
Assembly Standing Committee on Ways and Means
Senate Standing Committee on Revenue and Taxation
Senate Standing Committee on Appropriations
Joint Committee on the Arts
California Arts Council

LOS ANGELES COUNTY
Los Angeles County Board of Supervisors
Chief Administrative Officer
Department of Public Works
Department of Regional Planning
Fire Department
Sheriff Department

KERN COUNTY
Kern County Board of Supervisors
Department of Planning and Development Services
Public Works (Roads)
Fire Department
Sheriff Department

FACTS

UMBRELLAS:
How many in Japan (blue): 1340
How many in USA (yellow): 1760
Height including base: 6m
Diameter of Umbrellas: 8.66m
Weight of Umbrellas without base: 203.2kg
Fabric area supported by Umbrella: 59.3m^2

ALUMINIUM:
Diameter of Pole: 21.9cm
Length of Ribs: 4.77m
Size of Ribs: 9.5x5.7cm
Length of Strut: 2.27m
Diameter of Strut: 7.6cm

BASES:
How many steel-bases in USA: 1625
How many concrete-bases in USA: 135
How many steel-bases in Japan: 1205
How many concrete-bases in Japan: 35
How many river-bases in Japan: 100

TOTALS FOR BOTH JAPAN AND USA:
Paint: 7,600 litres
Total length of Poles: 17.7km
Total number of Ribs: 24,800
Total length of Ribs: 118.3km
Total number of Struts: 24,800
Total length of Struts: 56.3km
Total fabric purchased: 410,000m^2
Total number of pieces per Umbrella: 470
Total number of pieces per steel-base with anchors: 64
Total number of all pieces: 1,655,400